'That dog that did it. It died yesterday.'

'Ryan's dog? The bull terrier?'

'That's the one.' Dawson clicked his fingers. 'Went just like that.'

'I'm relieved to hear it. I still say it should have been put down. It was a monster.'

'That's what everyone says.'

'What happened to it?'

He shrugged his massive shoulders. 'It was just sort of running along the road, and suddenly it just kind of stopped, its eyes bulged out of his head and it gave this funny sort of yelp. And it died. That was it.'

'Good heavens. That was sudden. I wonder what caused it.'

'Dunno,' Dawson said. 'Maybe it was my Landrover going over the top of it. Anyway, mustn't hold you up. I know you're a busy man.'

Also in Arrow by Colin Bowles

FLYING BLIND
FLYING HAZZARD

HAZZARD IN THE AIR

Colin Bowles

ARROW BOOKS

Arrow Books Limited
62-65 Chandos Place, London WC2N 4NW

An imprint of Century Hutchinson Limited

London Melbourne Sydney Auckland
Johannesburg and agencies throughout
the world

First published in Great Britain in 1988
by Century Hutchinson Limited
Arrow edition 1989

Printed and bound in Great Britain by
Courier International Ltd, Tiptree, Essex

ISBN 0 09 959920 1

For Danny and Anne, for buying so many copies
of the first one

AUTHOR'S NOTE

The town of Preston does not officially exist. It is a composite of several West Australian towns.

The characters in this book are also purely fictional; it has not been my intention to portray anyone living or dead.

Some of the incidents are based on fact; and I would like to take the opportunity to thank Dr Richard Heazlewood for the reminiscences that contributed to several of the stories in this book. However I would resist suggestions that any of the men and women of the medical and law enforcement agencies of the Kimberley bear any resemblance to the rogues and scoundrels depicted in this book.

1

Diamond Jim wore the smell of death about him, I doubted that he would survive the flight to Preston.

He was an old man now; his medical record dated his birth *circa* 1900, but he could have been much older. The sparse strands of hair, plastered flat on the brown sheen of his skull were pure white, and the ravages of disease had hollowed his cheeks, outlining the contours of the bones, beneath the parchment-like skin. His false teeth had been removed at the hospital, and as they hoisted the stretcher into the cabin of the Cessna, he looked for all the world like a wizened brown monkey.

The legend of the man would outlive him. But now he looked utterly mortal.

'Soon have you back at Preston,' I told him, and squeezed his arm in re-assurance.

'Thanks young 'un,' he mumbled. He seemed about to say something else, but then perhaps he decided against the effort. He closed his eyes and turned his face away from the glare of the midday sun.

Joe Kennedy clambered in and settled himself behind the controls. 'Okay, doc?'

'Okay.'

The engines clattered and throbbed into life. I was about to slam shut the cabin door. It was then I saw the battered blue Holden weaving across the aerodrome towards us, its tyres ploughing an orange plume of dust into the air behind it. The driver was yelling and waving out of the open window. He was heading straight towards us.

'Wait a minute, Joe.'

'What's up?'

'I don't know. We'd better just wait a tick and see.'

The man seemed to be out of the car and running even before the car had skidded to a halt. The broad-rimmed hat flew into the dirt behind him. He ignored it. His belly wobbled inside his breeches as he ran, like some monstrous water-filled balloon.

'Doc,' he gasped. 'Is he there? He hasn't kicked orf, 'as he, the miserable bludger?'

'Who are you? What do you want?'

The man was breathless from exertion. He stared past me into the cabin. 'Jim!'

The old man twisted his head around at the sound of his name. He blinked into the glare, his forehead wrinkling to a frown. 'Who's that?'

'Jim, it's me, Thommo!'

'Thommo?'

The man was forced to yell at the top of his voice, over the roar of the engines. 'From Maley's, remember? We worked in the sheds together.'

I'd assumed that Thommo was an old pal of Jim's, come to say his goodbyes. I stood back and let him have his last few words to the old man.

'Thommo?' Jim repeated. He seemed to be having trouble recalling the friendship.

'Jim, you're going to cark it any minute. You might as well tell us. Where are the bloody diamonds, you miserable bastard?'

I realized, with disgust, what was going on. I shoved Thommo away from the plane and slammed the cabin door. I signalled for Joe to taxi onto the strip for take off. But Thommo wasn't easily deterred. He ran along-side the moving plane, beating on the cabin door and trying to press his face against the perspex of the rear window. He was still shouting, but his voice was drowned out by the throb of the Cessna's propellers.

Finally, exhausted, Thommo staggered and fell and was swallowed up in the cloud of ochre dust kicked up by the undercarriage. I looked down at my ailing patient. 'Sorry about that,' I muttered.

'It's all right,' Jim said. 'Happens to me all the time.'

Diamond Jim never made it to Preston. It happened ten minutes after we took off. There was no trauma; he simply let go.

I was kneeling in the rear of the cabin, checking his pulse and temperature. He had been sedated at the hospital before the flight, and there was little else to be done for him. He opened one eye and turned his head slightly. 'Come here, young 'un,' he muttered.

'What is it, Jim?'

'I'm off now.'

I thought he was delirious. 'Just rest.'

'Thanks for all your trouble.'

'It's right, Jim. Just close your eyes and take it easy.'

'I want you to have this.' The brown claw of his hand rose from the bed and pressed itself against my chest. I took his hand in mine and I felt it open and press something small and very hard into my palm. I looked down. It was a small, pure white diamond.

'Jim. It's a diamond!'

'Bloody lot of good they've done me.'

'You had them all along!'

His lips stretched into a toothless grin. ''Course I did.'

It came out of my mouth automatically. 'Where are the others?'

He looked at me for long moments and there was something behind those sad, grey-flecked eyes, a mixture of amusement and regret. He stared at me for what seemed like an eternity, then slowly closed his eyes. He muttered something that sounded like 'Darn well forgot,' and died.

'Yairs, well,' Clyde Westcott was saying, 'people have

been wondering what he did with those diamonds for over twenty-five years. No one's ever proved he had 'em, of course. They even tried to put him away once, him and his pals. Carted him all the way down to Perth for the trial, but the jury just laughed it out of court. Bit of a character, old Jim. Made some of those posh legal eagles look like right dills.'

'What's it all about?' I asked him. 'I've heard people mention it once or twice, but I've never heard the full story.' I was yet to tell anyone about the small diamond Jim had pressed into my palm. Although I had no thoughts of keeping it for myself, I was considering donating the proceeds of its sale to the Flying Doctor funds. After all, it seemed to me that that was what Jim had intended. But I also knew that there was some sort of controversy surrounding the diamonds, and that merely to confess its origin would be to awaken a slumbering monster.

Clyde put down his pencil, leaned back in his chair and turned down the volume on the transceiver. It was the afternoon galah session. A female voice was reciting the recipe for a chicken casserole. 'So you want the full story, do you?'

'Well, not every single detail perhaps but . . .'

Clyde wasn't listening. 'Well, let's see. It was 1942. Everyone was panickin'. The Japs had taken Singapore and then they seemed to be all over the place. New Guinea, Java, no one could stop 'em. It was Churchill's fault, of course, but that's another story. Still, no one ever thought they was goin' to bomb Australia. Just didn't seem real somehow. It was just wishful thinking – there was nothing to stop 'em. One day – in March, if I remember right – a squadron of Zeros attacked Broome. Shocking mess. Roebuck Bay was full of flying boats taking Dutch soldiers and their families down south from Indonesia. Dutch East Indies it was then.'

'I've been out to Roebuck at low tide. You can still see the wrecks of some of the Dorniers in the mud.'

'Yairs, they're still there. It was a terrible tragedy, you know. There was a lot of women an' kids on those planes. One poor Dutch bloke lost his whole family. The flying boats were sitting ducks. The fighters just went round and round the bay strafing the lot of 'em. Shocking loss of life. They reckon there was over a hundred killed that day. The ones who got away from the bullets got taken by the sharks. Terrible. Still, that's another story.'

'I know all about that.'

'All right, all right. Anyway, it was on the way back from the raid that the Japs came across this Dutch DC-3. It was carrying some more refugees from Bandoeng. They shot it down and it crash landed in Carnot Bay. The survivors got picked up a few days later.'

'So where do the diamonds come into it?'

'I'm coming to that bit,' Clyde growled. My habit of impatience was a continual source of irritation to him. The locals agreed you couldn't rush Clyde out of a burning building. 'The thing was, just as the plane was taking off from Java, somebody threw a brown paper parcel at the pilot and told him to get it out of the country. He threw it in the plane's safe and didn't think no more about it.'

'That was the diamonds.'

'Too right. Only a quarter of a million quids worth. Must have come from the Dutch Treasury in Bandoeng, everyone reckons. Anyhow, when the soldiers finaly got to the wreckage, the plane had broken up on the beach in a storm. There wasn't much of it left. And the diamonds had gone.'

'So how did Diamond Jim get mixed up in it?'

'Oh, gawd, give me a chance,' Clyde protested. 'What I was going to say, before I was so rudely inter-

11

rupted, was that no one knows how he got hold of them. He never did nothing much in his life. Bit of mining, bit of beachcombing. Maybe he just happened to be in the right place at the right time. Maybe the safe got busted open in the crash and the parcel of diamonds got washed up on the beach close by. All anyone knew was that Jim suddenly started to pay his bills at the hotel and the store – which was a remarkable event by itself – and he pays in *diamonds*. Well, the police pick him up and take him in for questioning and he tells them that he found these diamonds on the beach. Naturally, they ask him where the rest of 'em are, but Jim says there was only half a dozen and he's spent them all. That was his story, anyway.'

'No one believed him.'

''Course they didn't. Couldn't lie straight in bed, old Jim. But no one could prove anything.'

'Weren't some of the local aborigines found with some?'

'I was just coming to that,' Clyde snapped. 'Yairs, those diamonds kept showing up all right. Blokes was betting with 'em in card games and they found black-fellas up at Lombardina and Beagle Bay with eighteen carat stones big as a fingernail. One of them traded a stone worth twenty-five thousand pounds to a Chinese storekeeper for a tin of baked beans. They arrested the Chinaman in Perth trying to sell it to a jeweller.'

'So most people still reckon Jim had the rest of the diamonds?'

'He had 'em, all right. Probably buried 'em up on the peninsula. There's a fortune sitting in the ground somewhere, buried in an old tobacco tin, or something. Worth millions in today's money, they reckon. The irony of it was, there was nothing old Jim could do with 'em. He couldn't sell the diamonds, and he couldn't give 'em back 'cos he'd already said he didn't have 'em. They'd have chucked him in the slammer

12

and thrown away the key. Spent the rest of his life living in a shack on Roebuck Bay. Did a bit of beachcombing, working when he had to.'

'Maybe he was better off without the diamonds.'

'Yairs, well, maybe he was. Only trouble, people never left him alone. They was always onto him, especially when he got older. "Come on Jim, tell us where they are. They're no good to you now." That sort of thing.'

'No limit to greed, is there?'

'Nar, you're right there, Doc,' Clyde said, and he turned back to the radio. I headed for the door. 'By the way . . .'

'Hmm?'

Clyde gave me a sheepish grin. 'Did he say anything before he died?'

'Say anything? How do you mean?'

'Well, you know . . . like where he hid the diamonds?'

'Clyde . . .'

'Well, you were the last bloke to see him alive.'

The last bloke to see him alive. That sounded ominous. I sighed. 'Darn well forgot.'

'What?'

'Darn well forgot.'

'Well try and remember!'

'No, they were his last words.'

'And what was the question?'

Now it was my turn to look sheepish. 'I asked him where he hid the diamonds'.

Clyde smirked. 'You too, huh?'

'It just came up in the conversation.'

'And he said he forgot where he hid 'em.'

'Apparently.'

'Silly old bastard,' Clyde grunted. 'God rest his soul.'

2

Sam Noriko was one of those people that you like and dread all at once. He was a tiny fellow, with cheeks the colour of polished brass, and a big infectious grin that seemed never to disappear from his face. He looked much younger than his forty-two years. In fact he had been just nineteen years old when he had drunk the cup of ceremonial sake wine and joined the other pilots of the 'divine wind' on 16 April 1945 on the island of Kyushu near Okinawa. Behind the controls of a Zero loaded with high explosives he had attempted to fly his plane into the bridge of the American battleship *Missouri* – and missed. Rescued from the water, he had later been accepted as an immigrant to the United States, and had made his home in California, becoming one of only two kamikaze pilots to survive the Second World War.

This was my new pilot.

The arrival of a second pilot had been anticipated for some time. Our workload had been increasing and Joe had been flying too many hours. I wasn't sure what I'd been expecting but nothing would have prepared me for Sam.

But Sam had come prepared for us. As soon as he stepped off the plane and saw us standing together by the little hut that served as the airport terminal, he raised his right hand, waved, and screamed at the top of his voice: 'How are you going, you old pair of bastards!!'

It's impossible to describe the effect of an American accent on an Australian word that has itself been corrupted from its original English. We just stood there and stared.

Sam bounded over and vigorously shook my hand. 'Sam Noriko,' he said, grinning. He turned to Joe. 'You must be Mike Hubbard.'

'Hazzard,' I said, quickly. 'And it's not him. It's me.'

'Sorry, you old bastard,' Sam said.

'I'm Joe Kennedy.' They shook hands.

'Okay, how about I buy you two bastards a drink. My scream.'

'What?' Joe said.

'I think you mean your *shout*,' I told him.

'Yeah, that's it. My shout.'

Sam Noriko had flown 737s for Trans-Continental and Braniff but he had spent the last five years in a little town in the San Fernando valley in California. He had worked as a crop duster, a flying discipline that required consummate skill in manoeuvring a plane so close to the ground. Later he started his own flying school but soon after his fortieth birthday the spirit of adventure that had led him to the ranks of the kamikaze impelled him to sell the business and come to Australia. Or perhaps, as Joe suggested, it wasn't so much a spirit of adventure as a mid-life crisis.

Sam had taken the precaution of learning the language before he arrived. God alone knows what tome he had been studying, but the application of an Oriental mind and an American accent to an outdated manual of Australian colloquialisms produced spectacular results.

'Can we grab something to eat?' Sam chirped from the back of the Holden, as we drove along the corrugated dirt road into town. 'I'm so hungry I could eat a baby's bum through the crutch of a low flying duck.'

'What?' Joe said.

'Come on, don't come the raw shrimp with me,' Sam said. 'You know what I mean.'

'What does he mean?' Joe said, turning to me.

'You old bastard!' Sam chortled from the back seat, and gave Joe a playful slap between the shoulder blades.

Sam seemed to be under the impression that everyone in his new country called everyone else 'bastard'. I decided I should make an effort to enlighten him. 'You shouldn't use that word all the time you know, Sam.'

'That's right,' Joe added. 'You could get yourself into trouble.'

'Okay, cobbers!' Sam laughed, but I knew he didn't believe us. I knew the moment he entered the Union Hotel, looked around the saloon bar and yelled: 'Hey, what a lot of old bastards!'

I knew when he headed straight for the lavatories, yelling at us: 'Won't be long. Got to point Percy at the wife's best friend!'

And I knew when he yelled at Gordon, the big Scottish publican: 'Hey, you old Pommy bastard! I'm hungry! What about a knuckle sandwich?'

I turned to Joe. 'We've caught ourselves a live one here.'

Joe just closed his eyes and groaned. 'Just our luck. Just our bloody luck.'

It had never been my intention to antagonize Ken Ryan deliberately. I only went to his office that morning to remonstrate with him about an article he had written implying that the RFDS[1] Residence was being used as a hostel for itinerant aborigines. He was referring, of course, to George. I had inherited George from the previous incumbent. George slept on the verandah with

1. Royal Flying Doctor Service.

his pet emu, Ethel, and usually helped himself to whatever was in the fridge. In return he cooked, cleaned when he felt like it, and generaly made himself invaluable to a bachelor professional with little time or energy to do anything else. I was sure Ryan knew it too, but for some reason – probably his inate prejudice – he had decided to make trouble for me.

I found him in the hot and muddled little office of the *Preston Bugle*, a newspaper known locally as the Three Minute Silence, because it was reckoned that was all it took to read it. It was actually no more than half a dozen Xeroxed sheets, crudely stapled together. Occasionally stories were accompanied by photographs, but the reproduction was so poor it was impossible to distinguish any shade except white and black. Consequently a picture of two newlyweds would resemble Haley's comet flashing past a quarter moon. But people read it for the gossip.

Ryan was hunched over a typewriter at the back of the room, his desk littered with back copies of the newspaper, shiny black and white photographs and cigarette ash.

I stood by the reception desk and coughed. 'Mister Ryan.'

He span round in his chair. A cigarette clung to his bottom lip and the fleshy pouches below his eyes gave him the expression of a colicky bloodhound. 'Hubbard,' he said.

'Hazzard, Doctor Hazzard.'

'What's the trouble?'

'No trouble. I just want to have a talk with you about that article you wrote last week.'

Ryan grunted, a noise that could have indicated resignation or irritation. He had only lived in the town for a year, and had been publishing the *Bugle* for just six months, but he was already accustomed to receiving irate readers at his office. Ryan was a larrikin with an opinion on everything, and it was widely believed that he had started the newspaper simply as a means of broadcasting his prejudices. With a circulation of less than three thousand – half that during the Wet – the business was not a going concern, Ryan obtained most of his income from his fencing contracting business. He also operated the town's only taxi, from which source he derived much of the material for the *Bugle*'s gossip column.

Ryan's larrikinism had resulted in some extraordinary headlines. When a local man, known to have a rather large family, was accidentally shot in the leg on a hunting expedition, the incident made the front page. 'FATHER OF TEN SHOT, MISTAKEN FOR A RABBIT' screamed the banner headline. When the corpse of an elderly aborigine was found in the local cemetery – where he had apparently been accustomed to spending the night – it was just grist to the mill for Ryan: 'MAN FOUND DEAD IN GRAVEYARD'.

His prose did not lack for colour either. Commenting on a local controversy over the culling of pests, his editorial pronounced that 'galahs have to be stamped out for their own good', a statement that was repeated countless times in the Union Hotel the following week. The previous month he had everyone in the town scratching their heads when his lead article contained the information that 'five aborigines were arrested in relation to drinking offences this week, a 6% increase on last week'.

My usual reaction to an edition of the *Bugle* was a mixture of amusement, outrage and bewilderment. But in the current edition I felt that Ryan had gone too far. I intended to put the record straight.

'So – what's up, Doc?' he said, leering.

'You ran an article this week claiming I was running a hostelry for every itinerant native in the Kimberley.'

'I didn't say that.'

'You implied it.'

'If the cap fits.'

'It doesn't bloody fit and you know it. George is an invaluable assistant.'

'Oh, yes. Does he draw wages?'

'You know he doesn't.'

'He's a slave, then?'

I could feel myself getting angrier. 'Of course he's not a bloody slave.'

'He must be a non-paying guest, then.'

'I want you to publish an apology.'

'And what are you going to do if I don't?' He watched me between slitted eyes, the soggy remains of the cigarette clenched between his teeth, plumes of grey smoke enveloping his head.

'I'll sue,' I told him, bluffing.

'Fine. Sue me. You know my motto – publish and be damned.' He turned his back on me and continued typing.

I watched him, fists clenched. I realized there was nothing more I could do. I had had my first confrontation with a media baron . . . and I had lost.

3

Silence so complete, so utter, you could hear the fish breathe. The water of the billabong was flushed pink by the last rays of the sun reflecting on the cliffs of the gorge. I sensed a spirit of peace here; a cathedral sanctity to the hushed stillness between the high walls.

A darter flashed low across the surface of the water, landing with a flurry on the overhanging branch of a paperbark. Above us, two wedge-tailed kites floated on the air currents, two specks of dark gold on the late afternoon sun.

We talked in whispers; we had intruded on a silence undisturbed since these rocks first rose from the seabed millions of years past, during the birthing of this vast continent. I heard the swishing of wings as a startled flock of jabiru wheeled away above our heads.

We sat on the bank to wait. A single barramundi broke the surface of the water with a hollow plop, the concentric rings on the water leaving its tell-tale sign. George nodded his head, and the big brown eyes turned towards me.

'Better we fix that tackle behind the tree, boss,' he mumbled. 'Or damn fish crawl up the bank and eat it out of our hands.'

We'd had to borrow Clyde's Land-rover to get to Forsyth Gorge. We had turned off the Beef Road towards the jagged spires of black rocks, bouncing across a ridge of stone and boulder, devoid of green. We could have been on the moon. Then we followed the stony river bed – there was no trail into the gorge – through a cleft in the escarpment into a valley of pandanus palms and black rock pools, blanketed with water lilies.

'What you want, boss?' George had asked me, as he guided the Land-rover between the craters and pools. 'Barramundi, black bream or trevally?'

'Barramundi, George.'

'Yo-i,' he grinned. 'We get any damn small fella fish, we throw him back.'

I thought George was joking, but he was deadly serious. Two black bream were spared, and on our third attempt George's rod almost jerked from his hands as a giant barramundi took his bait. We saw it dance on the silver pool for a moment, then dive below the surface, its struggles churning the water to a boiling foam. George fought it for almost a quarter of an hour before reeling it in. It must have weighed over three pounds.

Later we lay in our sleeping bags staring at a brilliant white blaze of stars. In the outback the night is close enough to touch. The Southern Cross drips silver.

'Is this a sacred place, George?'

'No, boss.'

'Please don't call me boss any more.'

'Yo-i, boss.'

George had always called me that. After a time I had come to realize it wasn't as much a token of respect as a symbol of our differences. I surrendered my attempt to change it. We were, after all, very different.

It was a full moon. It hung over the lip of the gorge like a freshly minted medallion. 'You see face there, boss?' George asked.

'On the moon? Yes. Yes, I suppose it is a face. The silhouette of one, anyway.'

'The Worora they got a story. They say one time there was this man and this woman. They got im just one daughter and they love her too mus. They got im dog too, and this fella dog he take care of little girl.

Well they go walkabout one day and bimeby they camp near im flat country. Well father b'long this little girl he doan like this place, he tell im daughter 'Doan you go longa flat country, you stay close by.' But little girl, she proper cheeky one, she doan listen longa her father, she go longa flat country one day and this fella willy-willy come, catches girl, lift her right up, right up longa moon. Too bad, too mus. She bugger up properly. Every night that little dog longa her he howl at this fella moon, tell her come down longa her family again. But little girl she trapped longa that fella moon now. That face up there, that face longa that little girl.'

'Is that Dreamtime, George?'

'Yo-i, boss, that's Dreamtime.'

'Do you believe those stories?'

'Sure, boss.'

'As if it actually happened?'

George fell silent for a moment. Then he said: 'You believe in Virgin Mary, boss?'

'Well, sort of. I mean, I'm a doctor George. I don't think it actually happened that way. But I believe it on the *inside*.'

'That's how I believe Dreamtime. Maybe never happen. But I believe it orright – in here.' He tapped his chest with his finger.

'So we're a lot the same, aren't we? We just have different ways of understanding the world.'

He shook his head. 'We different orright.'

'Do you think so?'

'When white feller he got im land, he put up fence longa that bit of land. Blackfeller he doan put up no fence. He doan own that land. The land it own *him*. He come out of the land, and when he die, he go back to the land. Like this place. Nobody own this place. When whitefeller shadow fall on this rock here, little bit this place he already gone away.'

We fell silent. Soon I heard the deep rise and fall of

22

George's breathing. He was asleep. But I lay awake for hours, thinking.

It was my first flight with Sam.

'Now take it easy, Sam,' I warned him. 'Nothing fancy first time up.'

'Don't you worry,' Sam grinned. 'She'll be oranges.'

'Apples, Sam, apples.'

'Are you sure?'

'Sam, I've lived here all my life. I know the language. Trust me.'

A few minutes later we soared above the Stirling Sound, the muddy shallows of the tidal marshes seeping to the rich blues of the distant ocean waters. A beef ship threaded its way through the islands towards the port.

'Is that the *Missouri* down there?' Sam asked me.

'Banzai!' I must have turned pale because he immediately nudged me in the ribs with his elbow and leered. 'Only joking.'

'Sam, there's something you should know about me right now. I have no sense of humour.'

'Too bad,' he muttered. 'Too bad.'

Djilbunga Mission stood on the edge of the Great Sandy Desert, a muddle of stone and iron buildings shimmering and rippling on the haze. A Pallotine priest, David Sievebeck, ran the store and a schoolhouse that served the local Nygina community and the nomadic people who occasionally appeared at the mission for food or medicine.

The hospital was a square stone building with a corrugated iron roof. There was just one ward with four beds, a treatment room, an office that contained the vital transceiver, plus a kitchen and a dispensary. I usually visited the hospital about once every two months to check on regular patients and conduct a clinic.

Margaret Shenton was waiting for me at the airstrip that had been graded next to the mission. Margaret was the AIM[1] sister who ran the tiny hospital. She did it with pride and precision, as if she were running a city hospital. I had known Margaret since she had first arrived in the Kimberley; a sparrow of a woman with a big heart and impeccable manners.

Sam's first words to her: 'G'day, you old tart! Getting any lately?'

I thought Margaret was going to faint. Her face turned the colour of a sterile bandage. Her face twisted in a tight smile and she said, 'I'm fine thank you. How are you?' and she turned and led the way to the waiting Land-rover.

I grabbed Sam by the arm. 'Are you out of your mind?'

'What's wrong, cobber?'

'Look, I'm not your cobber. And that lady is *not* a tart. You don't talk to women that way in California, do you?'

He was going to say, 'But this is Australia,' and thought better of it. Instead he stammered: 'That's what they say in the Union.'

'Maybe, but the ladies that go in the Union Hotel aren't the sort of ladies running AIM hospitals. Okay? So you'd better apologize to her.'

'Okay, cobber.'

Margaret accepted Sam's mumbled apologies with some grace and chatted cheerfully about developments at the Mission since my last visit. One of her native nurses, Beryl, was pregnant. She would have to find a replacement. Limbunya had been badgering her to go to Preston to visit his daughter, whom I had taken to the Leprosarium some months before. And she had a

1. Australian Inland Mission.

new patient for me, an old prospector who had arrived at the mission the previous day - in a wheelbarrow.

'A *wheelbarrow?*'

'I'll tell you the story when we get inside.'

Margaret's two remaining nurses, known as Minnie and Maxie, were standing to attention on the verandah, as if ready to pass muster. I grinned at them as I got out. 'At ease, girls.'

'Yo-i, Doc,' Minnie shouted, revealing a beautiful set of powder white teeth. 'How's that Missus Hoagan, eh?'

I groaned. The Kimberley is three times the size of England with a tiny fraction of the population but it's almost impossible to do anything without everyone else knowing about it. I might as well have been living in a small town. Since the radio was the sole means of communication between the isolated and scattered communities, each conversation can have hundreds of eavesdroppers. Minnie was known to spend hours tuned in to the Flying Doctor waveband, learning of the lives and loves of people she had never met, and probably never would. I suppose it was like a soap opera with a living cast.

'Missus Hoagan is fine,' I mumbled.

'You bin marry her, yet?'

'No, not yet, not yet.'

'Why not, Doc?'

Why not indeed. I had asked myself that question many times. But Megan wouldn't give up the station and I wouldn't give up my job. We couldn't tie the knot until we had unravelled the Gordian tangle of our own priorities, I guessed.

Margaret spared me further interrogation. 'That's quite enough, Minnie,' she scolded. 'The doctor has work to do.'

'Say hi to Missus Hoagan for me,' Minnie shouted,

as I went inside. I promised I would, making a mental note to first tell Megan who Minnie was.

There were four live-in patients the day I arrived, so the hospital was considered full. There was a four-month-old baby with heatstroke, a young girl with a threatened miscarriage and a man with a spear wound in his thigh, the result of a ritual tribal punishment. In the fourth bed was Jock McStuart.

Jock sat bolt upright in the bed, his hands folded in his lap. In fact his hands were the first thing you noticed about him; they were huge, with palms calloused from heavy work, the colour and texture of an old saddlebag. He had wisps of long white hair, plastered flat across his scalp, and his teeth were square and brown and widely spaced, like tombstones in an abandoned church. But there was a dignity about him, in the carriage of his head and the thrust of his jaw.

He surveyed me imperiously down the length of his nose. 'There's nothing wrong with us,' he told me. 'We wish to leave now.'

I turned to Margaret in confusion. 'What does he mean "we?"'

'He always talks about himself that way. Don't ask me why. Claims to have blue blood in the family somewhere.'

'We are quite well now, thank you. We wish to discharge ourselves.'

'Perhaps you'd let me have a good look at you first,' I said.

'Yeah, shut up, you daft old bastard,' a voice said. I looked down. A pile of rags lying by the side of the bed began to rise from the floor of its own volition. It appeared that this was where it had spent the night. It held out a grimy paw.

'This is Mister Menzies,' Margaret told me.

'Just call me Bluey,' he said.

Bluey was a tall man, with a bush grey beard and a mop of grizzled hair. He didn't have a single tooth in his head, so that when he grinned it was like peering into a gloomy cave surrounded by a forest of spinifex. He had watery blue eyes and an expression of mischievous good humour. He pumped my hand in greeting.

'Who are you?'

'I'm Jock's mate,' Bluey said.

'He brought Jock here in his wheelbarrow,' Margaret added. 'Took him two days.'

I rapidly revised my first impression of Bluey. I shook his hand, 'A wheelbarrow? That was quite a feat, Bluey.'

'Weren't nuthin'. Me coat keeps out the worst of the heat.' He patted the heavy trenchcoat he wore over his torn shorts and filthy white singlet.

I stared at him. 'You mean you wear that all the time?'

Bluey rubbed a corner of the heavy garment between his finger and thumb. 'Wouldn't go anywhere without it. Keeps the sun orf.'

I looked at Margaret. She shrugged helplessly.

'What about us?' the voice from the bed protested.

'Pipe down,' Bluey said. 'He'll get to you in a minute, you rude old bugger.'

'Yes, won't be a moment, Mister McStuart.'

'New chum,' Bluey told me, in a whisper that could have been heard in the schoolhouse a hundred yards away. 'Only got here in 1910.'

'We are a descendant of the Duke of Wellington. We are not to be treated like one of the hoi polloi.'

'All right,' I sighed. 'Let's have a look at you.'

Jock had a heart murmur and high blood pressure.

'What happened?' I asked.

'He fell over,' Bluey said. 'Just like that. Groaned, and fell over.'

27

'We feel much better now,' Jock said.

Bluey scratched at the wiry tangle of his beard. 'Trouble is, the old bugger's getting old.'

'We are not old!'

'You're ancient.'

'We are only two years older than you!'

'Ten years, if it's a day.'

'All right, all right,' I said. 'That's enough. Blood pressure's high enough already. I won't be a moment. I want to talk to Sister Shenton.'

We went into the tiny office and I shut the door behind me.'Tell me about them,' I said.

'They've got this mine about twenty miles from here. Mica and felspar and a bit of gold, I gather. Not much though. They come to the mission about once a month to pick up stores. On foot, mind you. Then they walk all the way back again, with their wheelbarrow. Funny old pair. They're always arguing but they seem to be inseparable. You never see one of them without the other.'

'The old fella's pretty sick.'

She nodded. 'I know.'

'There's no point in treating him here. First chance he gets he'll go running back into the bush. I'd better take him back with me to Preston.'

'I hoped you would.'

I went back outside to talk to old Jock. 'Can I go home now?' he asked me.

I shook my head. 'Your blood pressure's way up, Mister McStuart. I'd like to take you to Preston with me for some tests.'

Bluey stared at me in horror. 'Just give him some medicine,' he said. 'He'll be right.'

'We are not going in that aeroplane,' Jock added. 'If God had meant us to fly, He would have given us wings.'

'You can't get proper care here. There aren't the facilities.'

'Well what's the point of having a hospital here then?'

I ignored the remark. 'Bluey can come along with you, if you like.'

Jock considered this a moment. 'How far is it by wheelbarrow?'

'I'm not pushing you all that bloody way,' Bluey protested. 'I'll bury you first.'

'That's a possibility,' I said. Jock bit his lip. 'I can't force you,' I added.

'We don't want to go.'

I knew from bitter experience that you can lead a horse to water but you can't make it take its tablets and look after itself. Besides, I had begun to learn that out here it wasn't possible to dictate terms; these people marched to a different drummer.

'All right. I can prescribe a course of treatment for you. But you'll have to come in to the clinic at least once a week.'

Old Jock smiled for the first time. 'Suits us,' he said with a sly look at Bluey. 'But, like he says, we aren't as young as we used to be. He'll have to push me in the 'barrow.'

4

The waters around Cape Leveque had shaded from the muddy brown waters of the Sound to the opaque blue-greens of the tropical ocean. As Sam brought the Cessna low over the water I could make out the silhouettes of turtles finning through the shallows.

Joe turned to Sam. 'Watch the crosswinds as you put her down.'

'She'll be oranges.'

'Apples, apples,' Joe muttered.

'That's right, apples,' Sam grinned. 'Sure is a strange language.'

'It's you that's strange,' Joe murmured. Sam didn't hear him.

There was no airstrip on Parrot Island. We were forced to land on a sandy strip near the Cape, two miles from the mangrove-fringed shore. Father Tom Pallemberg was waiting for us in a Land-rover.

'Good to see you, Mike,' the priest said, proffering an enormous brown paw. 'Who are these two fellows?'

Joe and Sam had just anchored the Cessna – a vital precaution in a country where a freak wind gust can turn a twin engine aircraft on its back in moments. I nodded to the two pilots now strolling across the strip to join us. 'You know Joe Kennedy. The other fellow's Sam Noriko. He's a new member of the team.'

Father Pallemberg shook Joe's hand. 'Pleased to meet you, Sam.'

Joe disengaged himself. 'I'm Joe. That's Sam.'

The priest squinted through the thick lenses of his spectacles, as though peering through a thick fog.

'Goodness, you're right. I'll have to get myself some new glasses. How do you do, Sam.'

Sam gripped his hand. 'How they hangin', you old bastard?'

There was a moment's silence. 'And the Lord be with you too,' the priest said, and led the way to the Land-rover.

We followed a deep, sandy track towards the coast, the bottle trees shimmering in the heat haze, appearing to gyrate on the plain like grotesque Turkish dancers. There was a dinghy waiting for us in the skirt of mangroves. We ferried through the swamp to a launch bobbing on the water a hundred yards offshore.

'You live there?' Sam said, pointing towards Parrot Island, a mile distant to the north.

Father Pallemberg squinted against the glare of the midday sun shimmering on the water, and started the diesel engine of the launch. 'Me and my flock.'

Sam looked puzzled. 'Flock of what?'

'My parish. The people of Parrot Island are my congregation now.'

'Father Pallemberg's retired,' I explained to Sam. 'He stays here because he wants to.'

'Lucky guy.' Parrot Island clung to the horizon, remote and inviting, fringed with green.

'It may seem so,' Father Pallemberg said. 'But the reality is much different. Our survival here is precarious. The shortage of food and medicine keeps us in constant crisis.'

'Then why live there?'

Father Pallemberg gave him a sad smile. 'Why, indeed . . .'

'The thing is, Sam,' I started to explain, 'most of the people on the island came here from Preston. They want to make their own living, instead of relying on government pensions. Father Pallemberg's trying to help them.'

'It was the Pastoral Industry Award that really broke these people,' the priest said, as he steered the launch through the shoals towards the island. 'I suppose it was well intended. It stipulated a minimum wage for all station hands. Until then almost every station employed native stockmen, and they lived in camps on the stations with their families. They didn't get paid very much – sometimes nothing – but they were all provided with food and clothing. It wasn't an ideal system by any means, but it was better than what they have now.'

'What was wrong with paying them a proper wage?'

'Well nothing – in theory. But it comes down to simple economics. The station managers can't afford to employ all these native hands any more. Suddenly they're all drifting into the towns. You must have seen them in Preston. All they do is hang around the government welfare office or sit in the park drinking their pensions away with cheap grog.'

'Why can't they just go back where they came from, then?' Sam asked.

'This is where they came from. But all the waterholes and kangaroo plains have been fenced off. Even if they weren't, a lot of the young blokes wouldn't know how to fish or hunt any more. They've forgotten. And most of the little kids will never learn. Why should they, when the government pays them money to do nothing? After all, it's hard work hunting down kangaroos with spears and boomerangs. That's the real tragedy of it. Believe me, you can destroy people quicker with money than you can with guns. It makes you want to weep.'

Sam scratched his head. 'So what's Parrot Island?'

'A few months ago two of the tribal elders made their way out here. They couldn't stand to watch what was happening in the towns. Some of the younger men

followed them. They want to try and support themselves, perhaps even sell some fish and their trochus
and turtle shell. They don't allow drink on the island
and the elders are trying to teach the old laws. It might
even work.'

'And what about you?'

'Me?' The old priest laughed. 'I'm just a silly old
fool who thinks he can help them.'

'He's spent every penny he has out here,' I added.
'He bought them this boat, and he made them a rain
tank. He's anything but a silly old fool.'

'The only problem is, he's blind as a bat,' Joe yelled,
pointing to a spot about a hundred yards in front of
the bows. 'Better grab the wheel, Mike, before he
drowns the lot of us.'

I looked up. We were heading straight for the reef
that skirted the island. 'I know what I'm doing,' the
priest said. 'I've done this trip hundreds of times.'

'You're heading straight for a reef,' I told him.

'Am I?'

I took the wheel and pulled the launch hard to port.
Father Pallemberg shuffled to the starboard rail and
leaned out. 'Goodness, I think you're right, young
man,' he said to Joe. 'With eyes like that, you ought
to be a pilot.'

Joe looked in my direction and scowled. 'Over ten
thousand flying hours and I end up drowning. That
would be just my luck.'

Father Pallemberg took off his spectacles and rubbed
them on his cotton shirt. 'I really must get a new pair,'
he sighed. 'I think I've worn these out.'

There were no parrots on Parrot Island. It was just the
first of many disappointments. The island was ringed
by mangroves, and the stench of them reached us long
before we pulled alongside the crumbling wooden jetty
that groped its way from the shore into the mud-stained

33

waters. The settlement on the island consisted of a jumble of ramshackle huts, constructed from corrugated iron and hessian and bark lost among a grove of ebony and wattle trees.

Father Pallemberg led the way. 'The biggest problem is the lack of fresh water,' he was saying. 'We need another tank but it's so very difficult getting materials over here.'

I thought of the diamond old Jim Palmer had pressed into my palm a few weeks ago. 'A little money perhaps.'

'Oh, a little money is what we need. But where is it going to come from?'

'Well, you never know,' I said.

Father Pallemberg looked puzzled. 'You know a mysterious benefactor?'

'The Lord works in mysterious ways.'

'I'm too old a buzzard to believe that. The Lord merely offers redemption. If you want private funding, you have to go to a bank.'

'We'll see.' I decided to say no more. The moral dilemma of the stolen diamond still tormented me. It was, after all, just one small diamond. Which was, in every probability, the property of the Netherlands government. They probably wouldn't miss it after all this time, I tried to tell myself.

Oh yes they would.

There was little time to explore the seemingly endless perspectives of my quandary. About a dozen of the island community waited for me outside the priest's ramshackle hut. There were five cases of trachoma, three tropical ulcers, a persistent headache, a broken finger that had already begun to knit of its own accord, and an ear infection.

'I'll leave you this medical kit,' I told the priest after I had finished the clinic. 'All the drugs are numbered. In future I'll be able to prescribe treatments for a lot of these cases over the radio. You'll just have to ensure that they take their medicines properly.'

'I'll do that,' he assured me.

Later, he showed me round the rest of the settlement. 'I think it will work, you know,' he said, his eyes burning with restless energy. 'Already a lot of the younger ones are forgetting about the grog. The older ones are teaching them how to make spears from the wattle and mangrove branches and how to catch the dugong. It's just a shame we're so far away from anywhere. Otherwise they could start their own fishing industry here.'

'If they can get through the first twelve months, I think it will work.'

'Yes, I know. If we can just find water . . .'

'I'm sure it will work out,' I told him with a confidence I didn't feel. I knew the odds were against them.

It had been my first visit to the island and I had been surprised at how inhospitable the place was, and yet how many Worora people had chosen to live there. I supposed that at least they felt that the island, poor as it was, belonged to them.

But my biggest surprise was reserved for when we were leaving the island. As the launch chugged across the straits separating us from the mainland, Father Pallemberg rested both brown and freckled arms on the wheel and assumed a solemn expression.

'Now tell me, young Michael, how's things between you and Megan?'

Word was getting around.

No, I didn't deliberately set out to antagonize Ken Ryan. But he definitely had it in mind to antagonize me.

The chickens were George's idea. He appeared at the screen door one morning holding a bantam rooster.

'What in God's name is that?' I asked.

35

'Chicken, boss,' George said, holding the bird up for my inspection. 'I bin won him in a poker game. Good, eh?'

'Get rid of him, George.'

He ignored me. 'This fella chook,' he said, chuckling. 'I reckon you me get some lubra chooks, then mebbe we grow 'im some more little chooks, mebbe fresh eggs every mornin' too. I look after 'em, no worries.'

'Definitely not.'

And so we got chickens. Four of them, the personal harem of Colonel Sanders, for that was what Sam christened him, and the name stuck. George built a coop out the back under the mango tree, and a new enterprise was born. Hazzard's Hatcheries, as it became known.

I should have known better. George's pet emu, Ethel, did not react with enthusiasm to the strange birds that had invaded her domain and she attacked the chicken wire with her beak. Twice the rooster escaped and had to be retrieved from a neighbour's property. But it was Colonel Sanders's fondness for reveille that was the major problem.

A couple of weeks after Hazzard's Hatcheries had been established I took George to one side. 'He's got to go,' I announced. 'I've had complaints from the neighbours.'

'What's trouble, boss?' he asked, the brown, innocent eyes growing wide.

'You know very well what the problem is. He sits on the coop and crows every morning at half past four. I know because I've got a luminous dial on my watch. Everyone in the street hates him. And so do I.'

George looked crestfallen. He had had great hopes for his first foray into husbandry. 'Okay, boss,' he said. 'No worries. I fix it.'

He fixed it by taping Colonel Sanders's beak with masking tape. The poor bird went crazy by dawn's early light and scrambled its way out of the coop through another hole in the wire that Ethel had obligingly created the previous evening. Evidence suggests that he escaped into the street where he was pursued by a neighbour's dog. He apparently fled, taking refuge under Mrs Denison's fibro. This was the worst place he could have gone.

Mrs Denison was a retired spinster, who harboured the belief that she was being persecuted for her adherence to the word of the Gospels, as propounded by *Watchtower*. Still dressed in her nightgown, she appeared on my doorstep at a few minutes to five and demanded that I retrieve my chicken.

'What chicken?' I mumbled, still drowsy with sleep.

'The one you put under my house!'

'I didn't put a chicken under your house.'

'I expected it of the others,' she told me, her frail old body rigid with indignation, 'but I didn't think you'd turn out to be a religious bigot too!'

I wondered if I was having a bad dream. 'I really don't know what you're talking about,' I stammered. And then I remembered Colonel Sanders.

'Oh, no,' I groaned. 'All right, Mrs Denison. I'll be right there.'

A few minutes later, wearing only shorts and a pair of thongs, I stumbled down the street after Mrs Denison in the semi-darkness, to retrieve my troublesome rooster. As we went the old lady yelled abuse in the direction of the other darkened houses in the street, accusing the sleeping occupants of being accomplices to this outrageous party trick.

When we got to her house, the damned bird was crowing with triumph on the back step. When it saw us it fled once more beneath the stanchions. With the tattered remnants of the masking tape still entwined around his beak, he fluttered and chortled with extravagant pomposity around the wooden posts. I got onto my hands and knees and tried to tempt him to emerge from his refuge by cooing at him, while Mrs Denison shone her torch into the gloom.

'It's because I won't have a blood transfusion, isn't it?' Mrs Denison yelled into my ear.

'Please keep your voice down. I'll have him out from under there in a moment.'

'He's possessed with a demon. It isn't natural for a chicken to hide under a house. He should be exorcized!'

'I think he's had enough exercise for one day,' I muttered and started to crawl towards him on my hands and knees. Colonel Sanders tried to take off, fluttered, hammered into the floorboards and a piling, and finally ran squawking into Mrs Denison's legs. She dropped the torch, yelling that she was being attacked by a devil. Lights began to flick on all the way all along the street.

Half an hour later Colonel Sanders was finally recaptured, to a smattering of applause from the throng of neighbours who had gathered in the first light to witness the spectacle. Embellishing the story later, I believe they named themselves 'Hazzard's Witnesses'. Mrs Denison had a coughing fit, lay down in her front garden and pretended to pass out.

Clutching the struggling bird under one arm I eventually returned home to berate George, whose culpability in my embarrassment was undeniable. But when I looked for him on the verandah, he had disappeared. He wisely went walkabout for a couple of days.

Once again I featured on the front page of the *Preston Bugle*. The article, recounting the morning's events, was headed: 'COCK GETS FLYING DOCTOR IN TROUBLE WITH SPINSTER.' It was too much.

'I want an apology!' I slammed the copy of the paper down on the front desk.

'What's wrong?' Ryan grunted, from behind a screen of tobacco smoke.

'That headline was constructed purposely to embarrass me! I don't know why you bothered reporting the incident anyway. It demonstrates deliberate malice.'

His forehead wrinkled into a frown. 'What's wrong with the headline.'

'It's an insulting innuendo.'

'Innuendo? Sounds like a ding's[1] name.'

'It has a double meaning.'

Ryan affected innocence. 'Does it?'

'You know it bloody well does.'

'In what way?' His face set like cement but his eyes twinkled with amusement. He was baiting me.

'You're not going to get away with this.'

'With what?'

I tore the paper in half and threw it at him. He didn't move. I went out, slamming the door.

I consoled myself with a small revenge. Colonel Sanders had planned his last great escape. That same night I roasted him with potatoes and a butternut pumpkin. He was finger lickin' good.

1. 'Ding' is an insulting Australian slang term meaning 'Italian'.

5

The community at Thalgo consisted of about seventy aborigines, who lived in a cluster of humpies and corrugated iron shacks about five miles from Djilbunga Mission. We set off in the Land-rover just before dawn, with the eastern sky stained to a burned orange, and the high, distant cliffs blue-black on the horizon. It was winter, and the morning air was cool. I slipped a thin woollen jersey over my shirt.

Joe and I had flown to the Mission the previous day for the clinic, and decided to stay there overnight. Margaret Shenton had asked me to come with her to visit Thalgo.

'I'm spending more and more of my time there,' she told me, as we bounced over the red corrugated dirt track. 'Half of the men have some sort of venereal disease. And almost all the women are either pregnant or suckling.'

'It's not a new problem.'

'It's getting out of hand at Thalgo.'

'We'll see what we can do.'

The problems of providing adequate medical care to the aboriginal population in the Kimberley were legion; the isolation of many of the communities, the nomadic nature of the people and the cultural barriers created by 'whitefeller' names and 'blackfeller' names had produced frustration and confusion ever since the aerial medical service was first created in the north-west. The situation was further exacerbated by the aborigines themselves, who had no concept of preventive medicine. It was the reason leprosy had scourged many of the tribes and why gonorrhoea and trachoma were rife.

Many natives did not even understand the process of conception.

Aware of the headache that Thalgo had become, I had come prepared that morning with a supply of condoms and a profound optimism that events would prove to be totaly unfounded.

A wisp of smoke drifted above the ironbarks when we reached Thalgo. As we climbed out of the Land-rover there was the usual chorus of yelps and whines from the dogs. There was the high-pitched squeal of an infant from one of the humpies and the fetid smell of neglect clung to the aroma of wood smoke. I felt depressed.

The clinic that morning was conducted from the back of the Land-rover. I discovered that Margaret had not over-stated her case. I counted twenty-three cases of gonorrhoea, ten of syphilis and ten new pregnancies. I had been depressed when I arrived; when the clinic had finished, I was desperate.

I decided it was time to introduce a little preventive medicine; so I sat on the tailboard of the Land-rover with the entire population of Thalgo gathered around and attempted to explain to them the mysteries of the rubber prophylactic.

'You must use this every time you . . . every time you . . .' What word did *they* use? I saw Margaret fold her arms and look in another direction. 'Every time you . . .' I decided a pantomime was in order. I jumped down from the back of the Land-rover and conveyed my meaning with a few well chosen movements. This brought the house down. But I decided they understood what I meant.

'This will stop you having babies and from getting sick.'

I carefully removed one from its silver wrapper, unrolled it and held it up for them all to see. Eyes rolled and pink mouths gaped open.

'You eat that one?' someone said.

'No, no, you don't eat it . . . What you do is you put it . . . you put it on your . . . Oh, God . . .'

I suddenly realized the nature of the task I had set for myself. I looked around desperately and on an impulse, picked up a large stick lying on the ground near the back wheel of the Land-rover. I planted it firmly in the ground and unrolled the condom along the twig. I pointed to the appropriate part of my own anatomy and drew more appreciative laughter.

'You must use one if you don't want to have a baby,' I repeated.

The old chief, Billy Jajaruru turned around and said something to the group in his own dialect. There was another howl of mirth.

Satisfied that I had made my point I began to distribute the condoms to all the men in the group. They held the boxes in their hands as if they were jewellery boxes. I felt like the Queen presenting George medals.

'Now old man,' I said to Billy. 'Will you make sure my instructions are carried out.'

'Yo-i,' Billy said. And then he uttered the two words every Australian fears the most: 'No worries.'

But I did worry. As I drove away from Thalgo that morning I worried a great deal. Perhaps I hadn't made it quite clear how those little rubber devices were to be used after all. I looked back once through the rear window of the Land-rover, but Billy and the rest of his people had disappeared in the cloud of orange dust chewed up by our rear wheels. The only thing that I could make out was a big stick by the side of the road with something like a sausage skin hanging on it. It looked strangely pathetic, like a totem for lost hopes, a wind-sock for the crows.

Inexplicably I felt another pall of depression settle over me.

'I'm sure we'll soon see an improvement at Thalgo,' Margaret said, in an effort to bolster my spirits.

'Yes, I'm sure we will,' I agreed, and stared out the window and moped all the way back to Djilbunga.

There is a theory that solitude breeds eccentricity. Certainly, the backblocks of Australia have more than their share of eccentric characters. The outback is a haven for those who seek to escape the conformity of the urban crush; the hermit prospectors, the quiet, rough men of the cattle country, the occasional fugitive from the law, and Remittance Men such as the Great Ballantyne.

I first met him the evening we returned from Parrot Island. Joe and I had adjourned to the Union Hotel for a beer with Clyde, who was celebrating his fifty-seventh birthday. There was a lot of talk around the bar of Diamond Jim and the fabled diamonds, and I also noticed there were a lot of curious glances directed towards me.

The behaviour of the publican, big Gordon McGlashen, struck me as even more curious. A middy of lager appeared on the bar in front of me. 'On the hoose,' Gordon said, and winked. 'For mae favourite customer.'

I accepted gratefully. Gordon was not known for his largesse. 'Thanks, Gordon.'

He turned to Joe and Clyde. 'Two middies for ye?'

'On the hoose, Bruce?' Joe said hopefully.

'What d'ye think I'm running here. Charity?'

'Why does he get free beer then?' Clyde protested.

'Yon doc's a friend of mine.' He plonked two glasses in front of them, splashing beer onto the counter. He held out his hand. 'Cough up.'

The reason for Gordon's generosity was soon apparent. After he had slammed the till shut, he leaned across the bar, tugging at the sleeve of my shirt to draw my head closer to his. In a booming whisper that could be heard on the other side of the hotel he asked me: 'Noo then, Doc. What did yon Jim say to ye before he passed on, may Guid rest his soul?'

The habitual hubbub of the saloon bar hushed to a whisper. I was aware of countless pairs of eyes turning in my direction. 'He thanked me for my trouble, Gordon.'

'Aye, sure he did. But what did he say aboot the *diamonds?*'

'Diamonds?'

'Ye ken what I'm on aboot, and don't pretend ye don't.'

'Keep your voice down!'

Gordon's eyes shone. 'He did tell ye something then?'

'No, of course he didn't.'

'He must hae said something.'

'He did. "Darn well forgot." '

Gordon frowned. 'What's that ye say?'

I shrugged. ' "Darn well forgot." '

Gordon shook my arm violently. Some of the beer spilled on the bar and started to drip onto my shoe. 'Then ye'll have to remember, laddie! It's important!'

'No, Gordon, *I* didn't forget. *He* did.'

Gordon straightened and frowned at me with disgust. 'That's the last free drink you're getting off me.'

'I didn't ask for it. You gave it to me.'

'Bluidy freeloader,' Gordon muttered and moved away. The hum of voices in the room resumed and everyone's attention returned to their own drinks and their own conversations. I breathed a sigh of relief.

Joe shook his head. 'If you ask me, there aren't any diamonds.'

'I agree with you, old boy. I think it's all a frightful hoax.'

I turned around. The speaker was a tall man with a shock of sandy hair and a beard as tangled and

44

unkempt as the coat of a wild goat. He wore a battered school blazer, rent along the seam under each arm so that a fetching tuft of hair protruded. There was a school tie around his shirtless neck. He had long army-issue khaki shorts and a pair of thongs. One bony white hand caressed an empty beer glass, the other was thrust into the pocket of the shorts, where it fidgeted aimlessly with its owner's crotch. I stared at him, speechless.

'My card,' the apparition said. He extracted his left hand from his shorts and fumbled in the breast pocket of the blazer. He handed me an elegantly embossed white card, with an heraldic coat of arms engraved in the left-hand corner in crimson and gold, bearing the legend:

Percival Stainforth Renfrew-Ballantyne
32nd Earl of Cumbria and Northumberland
469th in line for the throne
of Great Britain
the Empire
and Territories.

This was the Great Ballantyne.

'Looks like Tom Brown's nightmare,' Joe muttered.

'Pleased to meet you,' I stammered.

'Delighted, I'm sure,' Ballantyne said.

'This is Joe Kennedy and Clyde Westcott.'

They shook hands. 'What a splendid bunch of chaps. I think I shall be very happy here.'

'You've come here to live?' Joe said.

'Rented a dwelling next to the Flying Doctor, wouldn't you know? Can't imagine what one of these chappies actually looks like. Goggles and a first aid kit over his shoulder I should imagine. I'm just dying to meet ___.'

'And I'm sure he's just dying to meet you,' Joe said.

'He can't wait,' Clyde added.

It took Preston a few weeks to accept the Great Ballantyne, as he soon became known. His outrageous accent – I suspected that he exaggerated it for effect – and bizarre appearance initially alienated him. Further, he was a Remittance Man, one of that strange breed that may be discovered in exotic corners of the world, subsisting on a cheque that arrives at irregular intervals at the local post office from some distant country – usually England. This payment is almost always intended to assure the recipient's continued absence from the bosom of a family to whom his very existence is a costly embarrassment.

But the Great Ballantyne was the possessor of that indefinable quality known as charisma. After the initial shock had worn off, he became a local celebrity. He was fêted for his eccentricities and sought out by the town's larrikin element for his entertainment value. He would do anything for a bet. He even swallowed a live frog in the hotel lavatory for five dollars. He could eat anything. The live frog was followed by a double-or-nothing bet that saw him consume a pound of raw liver in four and a half minutes.

He quickly carved a niche for himself in local folklore. One afternoon he created a minor sensation by persuading Gordon to extend him credit at the bar, surrendering his false teeth as collateral.

The Great Ballantyne was capable of anything. One morning I woke at 3 a.m. to the sound of a trumpet rendition of the 'Mountains of Mourne'. The next morning he vaulted the fence and unashamedly helped himself to the contents of my refrigerator.

George was terrified of him, and assured me he was an evil spirit. Ethel, George's pet emu, took off at the very sight of him. Even the chickens stopped laying.

This was my new neighbour.

But the Great Ballantyne had one redeeming feature.

We were united in our enmity to Kevin Ryan, editor of the *Preston Bugle*.

Every Friday evening Ryan appeared at the front bar of the Union Hotel, distributed copies of his Xeroxed news-sheet to regular subscribers, and then perched himself on a stool at the end of the bar to imbibe three middies before heading home for his tea. His regular companion was an ancient bull terrier called Ruperta, named after Ryan's personal hero, Rupert Murdoch. She was a hideous-looking creature, with dirty cream-coloured fur, reminiscent of a lavatory wall, and obscene pink dugs that dragged along the ground as she walked. Her jaws would not have shamed a mako shark. The brute was universally feared and detested. She had savaged two small aboriginal children in the past six months but the local police had been unable – or unwilling – to have the beast destroyed.

The Great Ballantyne took an immediate dislike to the animal.

I was fortunate enough to be present the Friday afternoon that Ballantyne struck his first blow. When I arrived, Ryan was already at his post at the bar, and had settled down to read the fruits of his week's labours at his office. He had barely had time to read through his lead story when Gordon tapped him on the shoulder.

'Ah'll nae stand for that, Ryan. Get oot!'

Ryan looked up, bewildered. 'What's wrong?'

Gordon pointed to the floor a few feet from Ryan's stool, where his beloved Ruperta now lay in blissful repose. Ryan gaped at the distinctive tapered shape of the droppings now curled into a pile in the middle of the floor.

'What's that?'

'I ken what it is, and I'll nae put up with it. Tha's disgusting!'

'Too right,' Ryan agreed. 'You shouldn't allow animals in here.'

'Aye, I shouldna either,' Gordon said. 'So get oot!'

'Me?'

'An' take that filthy mongrel with ye!'

Ryan suddenly realized that his beloved Ruperta stood accused of the heinous deed. 'She didn't do that!'

'Ye're nae telling me *ye* did it?'

Ryan was flustered now. 'Of course I didn't do it. Neither did Ruperta!'

'I canna see any other dogs in the bar.'

'Ruperta's house-trained, you stupid Pommy bastard!'

The intake of breath from the audience of onlookers sounded like the hiss of a giant snake. Gordon McGlashen was one of the most physically formidable men I had ever seen. It was said that if he ever got on a horse, his feet would still drag on the ground. He had arms like sides of pork and a chest like a beer keg. He was generally slow to temper, but if there was one thing he couldn't tolerate, it was being called a Pom. He was Scottish, and proud of it.

Ryan immediately realized he had gone too far. His stool clattered to the floor and he started to retreat. He was too slow. Gordon's right fist connected with his nose, sending him sprawling backwards across the floor. Ruperta leaped to her feet, her teeth bared with murderous intent. She rushed at the bar, growling horribly, and attempted a leap at Gordon's throat. Fortunately the old beast was too short and too fat to succeed. Instead, she ran head first into the side of the jarrah bar with a hollow thud. After a half dozen further attempts, she staggered away, whimpering.

Ryan was still on his knees, shaking his head. A trickle of blood dribbled from his right nostril.

'Noo get out!' Gordon roared at him.

Ryan and his deadly pet both staggered outside.

48

Gordon grabbed Ryan's glass and tipped the rest of his beer into the slops. He stared at the pile of droppings on the floor. 'Bluidy disgustin'!' He turned towards the kitchen. 'Nellie! Come an' clear this up, will ye!'

'It's all right, old chap, I'll do it,' Ballantyne said and he strolled over to the pile of ordure, picked it up, and placed the unspeakable mess in the pocket of his blazer.

'Guid, ye're a sick mon, Ballantyne,' Gordon said, wrinkling his nose in disgust.

Ballantyne retrieved the brown muck from his pocket and held it under his nose. 'Oh, it's not so bad,' he said. 'Here, have a sniff.'

Gordon turned pale. 'Ye can get oot of mae bar, too.'

With a grin Ballantyne opened his fist and allowed the contents to drop onto the bar top. It bounced off onto the floor and splintered into three pieces. 'Plaster of Paris,' Ballantyne grinned. 'Made it myself this morning. You'd swear it was the real thing, wouldn't you?'

Gordon stared at him, stunned. Then he threw back his head and roared. The whole bar erupted with laughter. The Great Ballantyne didn't have to buy his own drinks for a week after that. It was the birth of a legend.

6

I was at the Flying Doctor Base, conducting my morning 'clinic' over the radio, when Bill Patterson's voice broke in.

'Six Tango X-ray. We have an emergency. Over.'

I knew the voice immediately. 'Banjo' was a popular man in the district, a big raw-boned man with a laugh you could hear from the other side of a cattle yard. He owned a small property called Coronation Downs, about a hundred miles away, where he lived with his wife Heather and their two children.

I flicked the transmit button on the transceiver, feeling Clyde's hot breath on the back of my neck. He hated anyone else operating his beloved radio when there was an emergency. 'Everyone off the air, please, we have an emergency call. Go ahead, Bill.'

For a few moments there was just the whine of the carrier wave and then Bill's voice came through the loudspeakers once more, as clear as if he had been standing in the hut there with us. 'Mike, it's Annie, I think she's got herself bit by a snake.'

Annie was three years old, the youngest of the two children. 'What are her symptoms, Bill? Over.'

'She seems okay at the moment. But she's got this funny looking graze on her leg.'

'Are you sure it's a snake bite?'

'Positive. Heather found her and the cats playing with this snake out in the yard. One of the cats is acting funny already. Like it's drunk or something.'

That sounded bad. 'Did you identify the snake, Bill? Over.'

'Christ, I dunno what it was. I didn't see it. But it

sounds like a taipan. Heather says she belted it with a stick and it slithered off. I've got the men out looking for it.'

'You say one of the cats got bitten?'

'Must of. Staggering all over the place. I reckon it's going to cark it, for sure.'

'What about Annie? No drowsiness. Can she talk clearly?'

'Like I said, she seems all right. But I'm worried about this graze on her leg.'

There was no doubt in my mind that we had to go. Besides, 'Banjo' was not the sort to panic for no reason.

'Okay, Bill,' I said. 'We're on our way. I'll give you an ETA when we're airborne.'

An hour later Joe and I landed at Coronation Downs. Bill was waiting for us on the strip in his battered old Ford tray-top. Heather, Annie and their nine-year-old son, Jack, were with him.

Annie sat quietly in the vehicle on Heather's lap. She resented this constraint, but I had instructed Bill to keep the leg immobile. The little girl waved to me as I stepped out of the cabin of the Cessna, 'Special treat, Mike?'

I'd fallen into the bad habit of bribing Annie with jelly babies during her periodic check-ups. Now, when-ever she saw the Flying Doctor aircraft, she expected nothing less than a chocolate bar.

'I'm sure I'll find you something,' I wheedled. 'If you'll let me look at your leg.'

'Better have a look at this first,' Bill said. He led me towards the rear of the tray-top and threw back the tarpaulin cover. The Pattersons' two cats lay under-neath, dead.

'What happened?'

'Had convulsions. I shot the other one to put it out of its misery. Annie doesn't know yet. She was bloody fond of those cats.'

'Let's hope they took most of the venom.'

'Too right.'

I pointed to the hessian sack that lay between the bodies of the two cats. 'What's in there?'

'Lenny found the snake round the back of the house. Must have crawled off there to die.'

I gingerly opened the sack and peered in. It was a taipan, the smallest and deadliest of Australian serpents. 'Good God.'

'Stupid bloody cats. Fancy havin' a tug of war with one of those rotten things.'

'Was Annie anywhere near the snake?'

'Heather reckons she had hold of the tail, if that's what you mean.'

The frowns on the faces of Bill and Heather were in sharp contrast to the behaviour of the two children. Jack sat behind the wheel of the Ford, imagining he was Jack Brabham, and Annie was engrossed in examining the contents of the glove box.

I produced a jelly bean from a pocket. 'Let's have a look at your leg now, Annie.'

She took the proferred sweet. 'Okay.'

It was only a small scratch, just above her left ankle. It could have been made by a stone or a sharp twig. It was by no means a typical invenomation mark. However, where a taipan is concerned, there is no margin for error.

I told Bill I would take Annie to Preston Hospital for observation.

'Can I come along?' Heather asked.

'Sure.' I turned to Annie. 'Want to come for a ride in our aeroplane?'

Annie considered a moment. 'Special treat?'

'How about a whole packet of jelly beans?'

'Fair enough,' Annie said and held out her arms for me to carry her to the waiting Cessna.

*

52

In ordinary circumstances it would have been an uneventful flight. Halfway back to Preston Annie was sitting happily in the rear of the cabin with Heather, having bolted down the packet of jelly beans soon after taking off from Coronation Downs. I noticed she had begun to doze off against Heather's arm.

'Getting drowsy,' I said to Heather.

'She normally has her morning nap about now.'

'I'd better check her pulse and temperature.'

Bill had thrown the hessian sack containing the taipan into the cabin, for a definite identification at the hospital. I picked up the sack and threw it into the rear of the cabin, so that I could get to the medical kit. It suddenly occurred to me that it felt much lighter than it should have.

I retrieved the sack and peered in. Empty.

My whole body felt suddenly numb, I froze. We were trapped in a tiny aircraft with one of the deadliest snakes in the world. I turned around and searched the cockpit desperately, expecting to see the terrible reptile coiling itself around Joe's leg, or worse, my own.

But I couldn't see it, and my panic increased. Where the hell could it hide?

I remembered a piece of bush lore someone had told me once. 'It doesn't matter how hard you hit a snake, it never dies till sundown.' I cursed Lenny for not decapitating the damned thing before he threw it in the bag. What were we going to do?

I must keep calm, I told myself. I took a deep breath and went to the front of the cockpit and sat down in the seat next to Joe. He must have sensed something was wrong, because he gave me a strange, twisted smile.

'You all right?'

'Mmm.'

'Look like you've just seen a ghost.'

I think I'm about to become one. 'Got a little problem,' I whispered.

Joe looked around. Annie was curled up asleep on Heather's lap, blissfully unaware of our predicament. Heather was stroking her hair, her attention concentrated on the child.

'So what's the problem?' Joe said.

'The snake's got out of the bag.'

Joe grinned. 'You're a wag.'

I shook my head. 'I'm serious.'

The grin melted away. Joe's larynx bobbed in his throat like a cork on the ocean. 'Well, that's it, then,' he said finally. 'We're all dead.'

'What the hell are we going to do?'

'What's the point?' Joe said, with typical faith in his own resilience. 'Might as well face it, we're finished.'

'It can't have just disappeared.' I looked under the seats, and on the cockpit floor, around the rudder controls.

'If it's wrapped round my ankle, I don't want to know. Just don't tell me.'

'Keep your voice down.'

Heather looked up. 'Everything all right, Mike?'

'Mmm.'

Joe's bulbous misshapen nose had flushed maroon, but the rest of his face had drained to the colour of chalk. 'Just my luck.'

'It must have slithered up the back. I'll go check.'

'It was nice knowing you.'

The initial shock had worn off. I decided that the thing to do was discover where the snake had hidden itself, and then make sure it stayed there. We could despatch it when we landed at Preston.

I got on my hands and knees and began to crawl to the rear of the cabin, peering under the front and rear seats.

'Mike?' Heather was staring at me in alarm. 'You sure everything's all right?'

I didn't answer her. I had just spotted the taipan.

Heather had brought a leather overnight bag onto the plane with her and had stowed it under her seat. The taipan had sought refuge inside. I could make out the tiny beads of its eyes peering back at me a few inches from Heather's legs, the sleek sinuous body coiled behind it. There was a sinister beauty to the creature that held me hypnotized for long moments.

'Mike, what are you doing?' Heather repeated.

What should I say to her? 'I think you might be more comfortable on the stretcher,' I suggested.

'Sorry?'

'The plane's overbalanced. We need more weight over the starboard side. Don't panic. Just get up very, very slowly, and go and lie down on the stretcher.'

'Oh, my God, there's something wrong with the plane, isn't there?'

'There's nothing wrong with the plane. It's just a precaution.'

'Then why are you on your hands and knees?'

'Please, Heather, just go and lie down on the stretcher.'

The poor woman's hands started to shake. 'We're going to crash, aren't we?'

I cursed myself. Why did I mention the damned plane? I'd just made things worse. 'No, we're not going to crash.' The taipan began to stir. 'Please get up.'

It was too much for Joe. 'For God's sake, Mike, just tell her the truth. Heather, there's a snake loose in the cabin.'

Heather clutched Annie to her chest. 'That as well?'

'No, not as well. We're not going to crash, but there is a snake. Now please, go and lie on the stretcher.'

Joe had put the plane on automatic pilot and

appeared next to me. 'Oh, my God,' he hissed. 'Look at that . . . it's bloody inches from her leg!'

The human animal has only two reactions to fear, basic instincts engraved in our genetic memory by the experiences of our primordial ancestors. Those reactions are fight and flight. Fainting is a means of 'flight' – the body's equivalent of 'playing dead' – and this was how Heather's physiology chose to cope.

I watched her eyes roll back in her head and she slumped down in her seat, unconscious, I turned to Joe. 'Oh, well done.'

'Now what are you going to do?'

'We'll have to move the bag.'

'It won't work. We've had it.'

'Thanks for those words of encouragement.' I crawled to the back of the cabin, where Joe kept his spare tools. I opened the kit and found what I was looking for, a long-handled crowbar.

I looked over my shoulder. We had just flown into a bank of cumulus, and the aircraft was cocooned in a ball of white fluff. For the moment the world consisted of our pilotless plane, and Joe on his hands and knees peering with great concentration under the seat of a snoring child.

An unusual situation.

'You're not going to attack it?' Joe said.

I didn't answer him. I hooked the end of the crowbar around the strap of the bag and slowly began to pull it towards me along the cabin floor, away from Heather's leg. I expected the taipan to strike. Instead, the snake's head disappeared out of sight inside the bag.

I manoeuvred the bag into the corner of the cabin.

'Now belt it with the crowbar,' Joe said.

'You've got to be kidding. If I miss, it'll go berserk. This thing's got more lives than a cat. It just proved that. I'll stay here and make sure it stays in the bag. You go fly your plane.'

A quarter of an hour later we landed at Preston aerodrome. The plane taxied to a halt, and Joe and I applied the principle of evacuating women and children first. After this had been done there followed a rather untidy scramble to be next out of the plane. It reflected no credit on either of us.

Heather and Annie were despatched ahead to the hospital. Then one of the MMA's fearless ground staff, a bear of a man called McManus, entered the cabin of the Cessna armed with a five-eighths spanner. We heard two loud thumps and the taipan was flung out of the rear cabin door and landed with a wet slap on the tarmac.

Joe strolled across, picked it up, and put it in his pocket. 'Lucky I'm not bothered about snakes,' he said.

'Where are you going with that?' I asked him.

'I'm going to go over and see Clyde. Drop it over his shoulder.'

'Wait on. He's terrified of snakes.'

Joe grinned. 'Yeah, I know.'

'Ratbag.'

McManus appeared at the door of the aircraft. 'Hey, Joe! What did you do with that snake?'

Joe tapped his pocket. 'Right here.'

'I haven't killed it yet!'

Joe leaped two feet off the ground and attempted to rip off his shorts in mid air. He fell on his backside, gibbering like a baboon. McManus threw back his head and roared.

'It's all right, Joe. Only kidding!'

Joe jumped to his feet, crimson with fury. 'You stupid bastard!' His indignation was spoiled by the fact that his shorts were hanging around his knees.

'Not bothered by snakes, eh?'

'Get stuffed,' Joe muttered and waddled back towards the hangar to sulk, re-buttoning his pants as he went.

After I'd driven home from the aerodrome I discovered that the excitement of the flight back from Coronation Downs had disturbed my usual routine. I adjourned to the outhouse with a copy of the *West Australian* clutched in my right hand.

I had barely settled myself inside when I became aware of movement somewhere by my ankles. I looked down and groaned in horror.

It was a snake, a large brown one, its slick cold body as thick as a man's wrist. It had wrapped itself around the base of the lavatory bowl, with its head out of sight somewhere behind me.

The paralysis that accompanied the shock lasted only an instant. Yelling with fright, I threw open the door and launched myself out of the dunny into the garden, where I fell flat on my face, tripped up by my own underpants. I must have looked ridiculous, but at that moment personal modesty was not a major consideration. I scrambled on my hands and knees across the sparse patch of buffalo grass and red dirt, and finished up with my back against the chicken coop, screaming.

'Anything wrong, old chap?'

It was Ballantyne. He leaned on the wire fence of the back garden and regarded me with casual interest.

'Snake,' I stammered, pointing to the outhouse.

'Really, old boy?' He climbed over the fence and peered inside. 'Good Lord, that's where you've been hiding!'

I staggered to my feet, suddenly conscious of my loss of dignity, and began to pull up my shorts. 'Stay away from it!'

'Why, old boy? He's quite harmless.'

'Is it?'

58

'This is Roger, old boy. He's a carpet snake. I keep him as a pet.' Ballantyne disappeared inside the outhouse. 'Roger, you naughty chap! How many times have I told you not to keep running away like that?'

'A pet?'

'Keeps the mice away, better than any cat,' Ballantyne said. 'Look, old chap, you're shaking like a leaf. Did he give you a bit of a fright?'

I went inside the house, found the brandy bottle and poured a large one. A few moments later Ballantyne appeared at the screen door with Roger clutched in his right fist.

'How about you pat him and make friends?' he suggested.

I threw the empty glass at the screen door. It shattered on the floor. Ballantyne ducked out of the way and disappeared. Happily, he took Roger with him.

Later that day, Annie developed signs of invenomation with slurred speech, droopy eyes and muscle weakness. She was treated with an antivenene and quickly recovered. It seemed that the two cats had absorbed the larger portion of the venom and the little girl had received just a minor dose. A day later she was back at Coronation Downs.

In fact her prognosis was brighter than for anyone else involved in the incident. Heather vowed never to fly again. Joe didn't speak to McManus for six months.

As for me, I was never able to use my own outhouse again. Ballantyne kindly offered to allow me to use his, until the phobia had abated. It never did.

7

We were sitting on the verandah of Clyde's red-roofed bungalow. The sun slipped quickly below the western horizon, a molten orange disc, leaving the lonely fingers of the mulga and claw-like branches of the boabs silhouetted against a violet-stained sky.

'Yairs, been quiet lately,' Clyde was saying, as he lovingly removed the tab from a can of beer, allowing the froth to spill onto the wooden boards, 'we haven't had any emergency calls since Banjo's girl got herself bit by that Joe Blake.'[1]

I settled back in the cane chair, and watched a noisy flock of galahs swoop down into the branches of the acacia tree behind the radio hut. The first night star appeared in the eastern sky, bright and very white, and it made me think about diamonds.

It had been over a month since old Jack had shoved that tiny diamond into my palm, and I still hadn't decided what to do with the damned thing. I had hidden it in a sock in my bedroom drawer, and there it had remained for the past weeks, while I grappled with my conscience. I had originally considered sending it to the Flying Doctor Headquarters in Melbourne, as an anonymous donation to the funds, and more recently I had toyed with pawning it in Perth, and giving the proceeds to Father Pallemberg and the Parrot Island community. But another small and nagging voice continued to gnaw at me. The diamond was, the voice told me, stolen property. The rightful owners were the Treasury Department of the Nether-

1. Australian rhyming slang for 'snake'.

lands government and if I traded the stone I would be breaking the law.

Worse, I might get caught.

Half a dozen times I had removed the stone from my drawer and resolved to pass it in to the authorities. Each time I hesitated, and finally replaced it in its hiding place. After all, I reasoned, it would serve a much better purpose on Parrot Island. And no one would ever find out. Or would they?

My tortured reflections were disturbed by Clyde, who shoved my elbow off the arm of the cane chair. 'I said, it's been very quiet lately,' he repeated.

'Sorry?'

'You aren't listenin' to me, are ya? Might as well drink on me bloody Pat.'

'Sorry, Clyde. Got things on my mind.'

'Want to talk about it?'

'It's a sort of . . . moral dilemma.'

Clyde raised an eyebrow. 'Oh, yeah.'

'I don't know what to do. I really don't.'

'It's nothing to do with that new nurse, is it?'

'New nurse?'

'Yairs, what's her name? Miss Goodluck.'

'Jane? Heavens, no. What do you think I am, a sex maniac?'

He shook his head, unwilling to give a definite answer, 'Yairs, well, you said it was a moral dilemma.'

'Not those sort of morals.'

Clyde took a long sip of beer. 'What sort of morals, then?'

'Well, supposing . . . and this is just a hypothetical situation . . .'

'Hyperthetricals? Is that some sort of disease?'

'Hypothetical. It means . . . well, it just means . . . it means something that could be real but it isn't.'

Clyde frowned. 'Like bullshit, you mean?'

'No, no.' I decided to start again. 'Look, just imagine

that someone had something that belonged to someone else, something that was given to him, or her, as a sort of gift, but he, or she, knew it belonged to someone else. Supposing also, he—'

'Or she.'

'Yes, or she, knew that person – or people – didn't really need it, and didn't even know he—'

'Or she.'

'Yes, or she, had this thing, and that someone else really needed it a lot more. Supposing too that these people weren't really . . . well, people, but a whole group of people who weren't the same people that lost the thing in the first place. They were completely different people, who had probably forgotten all about the thing the other people lost because it was such a long time ago. Now, if you were in that situation, what would you do?'

Clyde shuffled his feet and scratched his head. He took another sip of beer. 'Buggered if I understand the question,' he said at last.

'All right, let's put it this way. Do you think it's morally justified to accept stolen goods.'

'Ah, stolen goods,' Clyde said. He was on solid ground now. 'Of course not. If it's dishonest, you shouldn't do it. No doubt about it.'

'What if the thing that was actually stolen in the first place, wasn't actually stolen. It was just sort of . . . found.'

'Still wrong though, isn't it? It belongs to someone else.'

'What if the thing that was . . . that was found was found a long time ago, and the people who lost it had forgotten that they'd lost it. Because it was a long time ago.'

'If something belongs to someone else, you should always give it back.' Clyde look infuriatingly comfortable on the high moral ground. Especially as it was not unknown for him to slip off and get his boots wet occasionally himself, just like everyone else.

'So you reckon that this theoretical person ought to give this theoretically stolen thing back to whoever theoretically owns it.'

'Yes,' Clyde said, drained his beer, and gave a low, satisfied belch. 'Theoretically.'

'It's an interesting theory.'

'Now then, Mike, all theory aside – what have you nicked?'

'A diamond.'

Clyde's jaw fell open. 'Diamond Jim?' he whispered.

'He pressed a small diamond into my hand on the way back from Broome.'

'You never mentioned anything about this before.'

'I'm mentioning it now.'

'Gawd,' Clyde said and he stared at me for a long time, while he speculated on the possibilities. 'You're not gonna give it back, are ya?'

'But Clyde,' I stammered, 'you told me that keeping something that belonged to someone else was dishonest.'

'Yairs, well, I thought we were talking theatrically.'

'Theoretically.'

'Yairs, right.'

'So you think I should keep it?'

He scratched his chin. 'Yairs, well, I mean you didn't actually *take* it, did you? It was given to you. And Jim didn't steal it, he found it. Di'n't he? Anyway, it was all such a long time ago . . .'

One morning, during the clinic, Margaret Shenton raised the subject of Jock and Bluey. 'I'm worried about old Jock. He's deteriorating fast. Over.'

'When did you last see him?'

'I paid him a visit yesterday. He hadn't been in to

the hospital for a fortnight and so I got in the Land-rover and drove out to the mine.'

'What's his condition?'

'He wouldn't let me examine him. But he looked terrible. He's still working down the mine with Bluey.'

'We're due to come out to Djilbunga next Friday. We'll pay him a visit then.'

'Thanks, Doctor. Perhaps he'll listen to you.'

'I doubt it, but it's worth a try. Over.'

'Well, there it is.'

'They *live* there?'

'For the past ten years, they tell me.'

There were two shacks, assembled from hessian sacks, packing cases and bits of old tin. They had been built under the shade of a stunted paperbark. A long bamboo pole stood betwen the two shacks, from the top of which fluttered a pair of crimson underpants, presumably the family standard of those in residence. A hundred yards further on, I could make out a narrow, rocky gully and the black maw of a cave. A wooden sign, hand-painted, announced we had arrived at the 'CLONDIKE'.

There was an air of desolation about the place. A piece of loose cardboard flapped in the hot wind. It appeared to be deserted.

It had taken almost two hours to cover the twenty miles to the site, along rutted and barely discernible tracks on the plains. Twice the rear wheels had bogged in soft sand. By the time we arrived we were exhausted, our shirts sodden with sweat.

I climbed down from the Land-rover, squinting against the bright sun and the sudden attentions of the bush flies. 'Are they here?'

'They'll be around somewhere,' Margaret said.

'I couldn't imagine staying here overnight, never mind living here for ten years.'

Margaret shrugged. 'Takes all sorts.'

'Is the mine worth it?'

'The pair of them talk about the place like it's the Transvaal, but I should think they barely make a living out of it.'

We made our way towards the larger of the two shacks, cutting a swathe through the clouds of tiny bush flies with our flapping hands. It was the reason we didn't see the old Lee Enfield rifle pointed at us from between the flaps of hessian until we were almost on top of it.

Margaret saw it first. She put out a hand and grabbed my arm. 'Wait.'

'What is it?'

She pointed towards the 'door' of the shack. I saw the muzzle of the rifle following our progress. 'Good God.'

'Jock, it's me,' Margaret called out. 'Sister Shenton, I've brought Doctor Hazzard with me!'

We waited. A head appeared from behind the hessian drapes, slow and suspicious, like a turtle emerging from its shell. It was Jock. The sparse silver strands of his hair hung about his face like blackboy leaves, and his face was covered with a thick layer of stubble. Beneath the stubble his face was the colour of chalk.

'We weren't expecting visitors,' he said, lowering his rifle. 'We thought you were claim-jumpers.'

'Put the rifle away, Jock,' Margaret said. 'It's dangerous waving guns about.'

'This is a highly desirable property. We have to be careful.'

'Didn't anyone ever tell you that guns were dangerous.'

'We thought they were meant to be.'

Margaret sighed. 'We came to see how you were.'

'We're fine. Come on in, we'll put the kettle on.'

The inside of the shack was every bit as luxurious

as the exterior. An upturned wooden box and two old beer crates served as table and chairs. The kitchen consisted of a portable camp stove and two cracked enamel plates, still stained from that morning's breakfast. A Zane Grey paperback and a single volume of the Encyclopaedia Brittanica stood side by side on the 'bookshelf', an upturned orange crate. Two metal cots stood one on each side of the room.

'You sleep in here together?' I asked.

'We like the company.'

'What's the other shack used for?'

'Guests.'

I moved further into the room and cracked my head on the hurricane lamp that was suspended from the ceiling.

'Have a seat,' Jock offered, indicating the beer crates.

We sat down. 'Haven't seen you at the clinic for your medication,' Margaret said.

'We've been busy.'

'How have you been?'

'We're in the pinnacle of health,' Jock said, and busied himself with the tea, putting half a teaspoon of black leaves from a tin into a blackened billy and putting it on the stove. The exertion brought on a wheezing fit, and he started to topple backwards. I sprang to my feet and grabbed him.

'You'd better lie down on the cot,' I told him.

Jock was a very sick man. He had lost weight, and the flesh on his face had fallen away, outlining the shape of his skull. He wore just a pair of tattered khaki shorts, and his skin was pale and translucent.

'Where's Bluey?' I asked him.

'Down the mine,' Jock said. 'We told him he'd have to work on his own today.'

At that moment the hessian flap at the doorway of the tent burst open and Bluey made his entrance. He was still wearing the woollen overcoat and he had a leather bush hat pulled down over his ears, beer bottle tops tied to the brim with string to discourage the flies.

Jock looked up from the bed. 'Speak of the Devil and he's sure to appear.'

Bluey surveyed the scene with a frown of irritation. 'You lying down again, you old bastard?'

'Go fly a kite, you colonial halfwit.'

'Useless old bugger.'

I stood up and took Bluey by the arm. 'Steady on, Bluey. Your pal's a sick man.'

'Nothin' wrong with 'im. He's puttin' it on.' But I saw a flicker of doubt cloud his eyes.

'I want to take him back to Preston with me. He needs proper care.'

Bluey's jaw set in a grim line. 'He won't go.'

'He must.'

'What are you whispering about over there?' Jock said, trying to raise himself on his elbows. 'We don't like whisperers.'

'Shut up and mind your own business, you silly old bugger!' Bluey told him.

I went back to the cot where Jock was lying and sat down. 'Jock, you've got to come with us to the hospital. We have to find out what's wrong with you.'

'There's nothing wrong with us.'

'Don't contradict the doctor, you old buzzard,' Bluey said.

'We won't go,' Jock said. 'We don't like the city.'

'It's not the city, Jock. Preston is hardly a city.'

'We won't go.'

It was Bluey who resolved the situation. He came to stand by the bed and leaned over so that his face was just a few inches from Jock's. 'If the doc says you've got to go, you're goin',' Bluey said. 'Even if I have to take you in the barra'.'

Jock glared at him in defiance. 'Only if you come with me,' he whispered.

'Of course I'm coming with you, you daft old fool. You don't think I'd let you go to the city on your own?'

Jock gave a long sigh and closed his eyes. 'Oh, bugger it, then,' he said finally. 'We aquiesce.'

'You what?' Bluey said.

'It means he agrees,' I said. 'Let's pack his things and we'll take him out to the truck.'

Bluey became a familiar sight around the town for the next couple of weeks. I often saw him shuffling along the road in his bulky overcoat, usually on his 'milk run' between the hotel and the general store, engaged in a vain attempt to extend his credit at these establishments. Someone in the hospital administration had taken pity on him, and he had been provided with a bed on the verandah of the hospital, so that he could remain with his old friend. They argued and abused each other incessantly, and Jock seemed to rally. He began to put on weight again and the ghostly pallor in his cheeks disappeared.

But the long-term prognosis for the old prospector was not good. His diseased heart required rest and a proper diet, and it was unlikely that he would survive very long if he returned to the mine.

One day I broached the subject with Bluey on the verandah of the hospital. It was a warm winter day, the sky a pale and watery blue, and the Blue Mountain parrots were playing and squawking in the mango trees.

'This isn't the place for a sick man,' Bluey was saying. 'He needs to get back to familiar surroundings.'

'What he needs is someone to take care of him.'

Bluey grunted and folded his arms. 'I take care of him.'

'In your own way, sure. But that mine's not the ideal place for a sick man.'

'It's homely.'

For a moment I was too speechless to answer. I thought I'd try a different tack. 'Has he got any relations? Someone he can stay with for a while?'

'Not that I know of. Maybe he's got some in the Old Country. He's a new chum, you know. Only been out here fifty-four years.' Then, as an afterthought, he added. 'He's like me. Spent his life looking for the 'ole where the sun goes down. He wouldn't know any of his family now if he fell over one of 'em in a dry creek.'

I didn't fare much better with Jock himself. When I went to visit him I found him sitting bolt upright in his bed reading a newspaper. 'Who's this Nixon fella?' he demanded.

'Nixon?' I assumed he was referring to one of the doctors. 'I don't know any Nixon.'

He slapped the front page of the newspaper with his index finger. 'Says here the President of America is a bloke called Nixon.'

'That's right, Jock. He was voted in last year.'

'What happened to Truman?'

'Truman?'

'You know, Harry Truman. What's the matter, don't you keep up with what's going on in the world?'

'Truman stepped down in 1952.'

Jock looked at me as if I'd gone mad. He folded the newspaper and put it on his bedside table. 'We'll have to discuss this with someone else,' he said. 'You obviously don't know what you're talking about.'

I decided not to pursue the conversation. 'Jock, the doctors here tell me that you've asked to be discharged.'

'We don't like it here. It's too . . .' He looked out of the window at the green lawns and the mango trees, '. . . arid.'

'Jock, you can't go back to the mine.'

'We feel fine, too. When can we leave?'

'You have a disease of the heart muscle. You have to take it easy from now on. Did you hear me?'

Jock folded his hands on his lap and studied them with intense concentration. 'We're worried about claim-jumpers, you know. That's a valuable property we have. We're going to make a major discovery any day now. We are thinking of informing the stock exchange.'

'You can't go back to the mine.'

Jock laid his head on the pillow and closed his eyes. 'We think we're ready for a short rest now,' he said, and went to sleep.

The next day Jock disappeared from the hospital. The hospital staff searched the grounds but there was no sign of the old man. Bluey had gone too.

There is no law preventing a patient discharging himself from hospital. But the hospital administrators were concerned about the two old men. Jock had been prescribed a course of drugs to keep his condition in check, and the doctors feared his condition would quickly deteriorate once more without them. But there was another, more immediate concern. Where could they go?

The question was answered late that afternoon when Constable Regan came across a strange sight five miles out of town on the road to Benowra Crossing. It was another warm winter's day, with temperatures in the mid-eighties, so he was surprised to see someone travelling the road on foot, especially wearing a thick woollen overcoat. Regan stopped to make a further investigation.

It was Bluey. He was pushing a wheelbarrow. In the wheelbarrow was old Jock.

'Where do you think you're goin'?' Regan said.

'Back to the mine,' Bluey said, and he kept walking.

'We have to get there before the claim-jumpers take over the place,' Jock shouted from the front of the wheelbarrow.

There was nothing to be done. Regan brought them back to Preston Hospital and next morning I flew them back to Djilbunga Mission.

I never saw either of them again. Jock took his medicine with him, and promised to report regularly to Margaret Shenton's AIM clinic, but I didn't hold out too much hope that he would see the Wet.

Sure enough, I got a radio message from Margaret a couple of weeks later to tell me that old Jock had died. But I didn't get the full story until my next visit.

'Bluey just walked in one day,' Margaret told me, 'all on his own. I knew what had happened straight away.'

' "Jock's dead," he said, and then he just sort of slumped down onto the floor. He was still wearing that stupid overcoat, and he looked exhausted. Of course, I didn't realize why. Not straight away.

' "I'll go and bring him in", I said, thinking he'd left Jock's body out at the mine.

' "No need to," Bluey said. "I brought him in with me. He's out the front, on the 'barra."

'I was horrified. It would have taken him at least two days to walk all the way to the Mission with Jock's corpse draped across his wheelbarrow. "Bluey," I said, "he'll stink to high heaven."

'I'll never forget the look on his face. "What do you take me for?" he said. "I wasn't born yesterdie. I gutted him first."

'Of course, I thought he was joking. But I went outside and he was right. He had.

'I asked him why he did it. All he said was: "Well, that's what friends are for." '

8

Progress advances inexorably. The north-west was growing, and business for the RFDS at Preston increased too. In an effort to improve the medical services to the Kimberley further, the Melbourne headquarters decided it was time that I had some assistance. A nurse arrived at Preston Hospital from Perth, and was rostered for flight duty with the Aerial Ambulance.

Joe didn't like the idea at all. He stood by the wing of the Cessna, tapping his foot with impatience. 'She's late.'

'She's not late. We're ten minutes early.'

'Not being early is being late.'

'Don't you think that's a bit unreasonable?'

Joe scowled and began to drum on the fuselage with the fingers of his right hand. 'Don't like flying with women. They're bad luck.'

'Rubbish.'

'She'll just make the plane heavier.'

I decided there was no point continuing with the conversation. I looked beyond Joe's shoulder to the hangar and caught my breath. A vision in white appeared to float across the shimmering tarmac towards us. It was our new nursing sister.

She was the most classically beautiful woman I had ever seen. She was tall, with platinum blonde hair that she wore pinned up under her nurse's cap. She had an oval face with piercing violet eyes, accentuated by high cheekbones. She moved with an almost fluid grace, like a model. I had seen her a couple of times over at the hospital and each time the sight of her had made me catch my breath.

She stopped a few yards away and smiled.

'Nurses! All sexless automatons anyway.'

'Joe . . .'

'They're all right in a hospital I suppose but in a plane they'll just get in the way.'

'Joe . . .'

'Never met a woman yet who's not bossy, overbearing and opinionated. It'll ruin the harmony.'

'Joe, just a minute . . .'

'You need initiative and . . . well, let's face it, intelligence. How many intelligent nurses do you know?'

'Quite a few, Joe, and I–'

'Nurses are just like worker bees. Better left in the hive.'

'Jane Goodluck,' the vision said, holding out a hand. 'You're Doctor Hazzard.'

I shook her hand. She turned to Joe. 'And you must be Joe Kennedy.'

'Buzz, buzz,' I whispered.

I thought Joe was about to faint. He rocked back on his heels against the rear cabin door, and sweat erupted on his forehead like a rash of tiny blisters. His cheeks and his nose flushed crimson as his face twisted into a sickly grin. 'Ngnngg,' he said.

I knew she had heard every word Joe had said, but she made no attempt to take advantage of his embarrassment. She flashed a warm smile. 'I've always been a bit nervous about flying,' she told him. 'But they tell me you're a wonderful pilot.'

Joe continued his impersonation of a man having a seizure, 'Ngnnngg.'

I looked at my watch. 'Better get going. We've got three clinics today.' I held open the cabin door. 'Off we go. Good luck, Goodluck.'

She got in. I turned to Joe. 'Sexless automatons, huh?'

'Why didn't you tell me she was there?'

'Sorry. She just zoomed out of the hive before I had the chance.'

'Just my luck,' Joe groaned and climbed in to the plane. He muttered to himself all the way to Brookton.

The first clinic that morning was at Brookton. Sean was waiting to meet us at the airstrip in the blue Holden utility. He was employed at the station as a helicopter pilot. He had worked for the Service as a relief pilot for a few months, and I knew him well enough by now to have a great deal of respect for his flying skill and none at all for him.

I clambered out of the cabin and hopped down onto the hard red dirt. Sean was already running to meet us. 'G'day, Sean.'

He ignored me. Instead he raced to the cabin door of the Cessna to help Nurse Goodluck out of the plane. 'Sean Thompson. I'm second in charge at Brookton,' he lied.

'Hello,' Jane said.

'Are you the new flight sister? They said you were a stunner.'

Joe appeared under the wing. 'Knock it off, Sean. You're dribbling on her uniform.'

Sean ignored him. 'The transport's this way. Not a limousine exactly.'

He carried her medical kit to the ute, opened the passenger door and helped her inside. 'I think I'm going to chuck,' Joe murmured in my car.

'Me too.'

While Joe secured the Cessna I hauled my medical kit out of the plane and ambled across to the waiting utility. Sean was already behind the wheel, pouring on the charm like a hot, sweet syrup.

'Mind giving us a lift as well?'

The sarcasm was lost on Sean. 'Yeah, all right,' he said.

74

I got into the front seat next to Jane. 'How's Megan?' I asked Sean.

'She's working in the yards.'

'Will I see her later?'

He shrugged, and his face assumed an expression of childlike innocence. 'She didn't mention anything. Did you want to see her about anything in particular?'

'It doesn't matter.'

'You know how it goes, Mike. Out of sight, out of mind.'

Joe had finished securing the guy ropes to the Cessna. He threw open the passenger door. 'Sorry Joe,' Sean told him. 'No room. You'd better hop in the tray.'

'Just my bloody luck,' Joe muttered and clambered on the back of the ute. Sean threw the gears into first and the clutch sprang back off the floor with a jolt. The rear tyres threw a spray of gravel into the air as we took off and there was a loud bang as Joe landed face first on the tray.

Sean gunned through the gears and we went hurtling along the red dirt towards Brookton. Sean gripped the wheel, grinning like a banshee.

Joe clung to the tray the whole way, his head bouncing against the metal. Once he looked round at me in the cabin, and yelled something that was lost in the roar of the old motor. But I could guess what it was. 'Just my luck.'

If Jane was impressed by Sean's virtuoso performance at the wheel that morning, she didn't show it. When she climbed up the steps at Brookton homestead she clung to the guardrail, and I noticed that her hands were shaking.

'Does he always drive like that?' she whispered to me.

'You know how it is,' I whispered. 'He was in Vietnam.' She seemed to understand.

75

It was a baptism of fire for my new assistant. We set up our mobile clinic in the homestead kitchen as usual, and prepared to treat the usual assortment of sprains, pains and infections that were common at station clinics. But that morning was by no means an ordinary one.

Our first customer was Wayne, a fresh-faced teenager no more than eighteen years old. He'd come to the Kimberley from the backblocks of Victoria, where his father was a shearer. He hadn't been in the northwest more than three months. His appearance was generally unremarkable except for the large blue and white striped football sock he wore tied around his throat.

The smell was appalling. Out of the corner of my eye I saw Jane turn her head away and pretend to cough into a handkerchief. 'What can we do for you?' I said.

'It's me froat, Doc.'

'Your throat?'

'Bloody sore. Oh, sorry, miss.'

'I'll have a look at it. But . . . you'd better take the sock off first.'

Wayne shook his head. 'Can't do that. The Gunner reckons an old sock is the go for sore throats.'

'The Gunner?'

'The new cook.'

'I'm sorry, Wayne, but if you want me to look at your throat, I'll have to ask you to remove the sock.'

Wayne reluctantly untied it and tucked it into the back pocket of his jeans. I turned to Jane. 'Want to take over?'

She gave the youth a quick examination. 'Looks like a streptococcal infection,' she said. 'Some penicillin tablets should clear it up.'

I checked Wayne myself and agreed with the diagnosis. 'It's not serious,' I told him. 'I'll put you on a course of antibiotics.'

'What about the sock. Better leave that on, eh?'

'The sock?'

'Can't hurt, I guess.'

'If I were you, I'd throw it away. It stinks.'

Wayne scratched his head. He looked disappointed. 'The Gunner fixed up Macka's sore throat this way.'

'It probably would have cleared up on its own. You'll have to take these tablets to clear up that infection.'

Wayne shrugged, got to his feet and shuffled outside. I watched him walk across the compound, pull the dirty sock out from his back pocket and begin to retie it around his neck.

'Who's the Gunner?' Jane asked me when he had gone.

'The cook. They call him the Gunner because he's always gunna do things. Always gunna make custard, always gunna make rice pudding. He never does, from what I gather. They get the same stuff every night.'

'How long has he been playing witch doctor?'

'First I've heard of it. But then, he hasn't been here long.'

The odour of Wayne's old sock may have been unpleasant, but it was a garden of jasmine blossom compared to the odour that accompanied our next patient into the room. Jeff was not much older than Wayne, his face pocked with juvenile acne, and his chin sprouting tufts of long blond hairs in a mockery of a beard. He complained of a fever.

The smell of decay that clung to him concerned me more than his temperature, which was only a little higher than normal. There was no obvious reason for the appalling miasma, a stench so bad that I thought I was going to gag. Jeff seemed quite unaware of it.

'Well, see, Doc, I've been feelin' real crook, I mean I just been breaking out in sweats and everythin', and when I woke up this mornin' the sheets were soaked. Christ, I dunno, I reckon . . .'

I decided to halt the litany of complaint while I still had fresh air in my lungs. 'Wait a minute, son. What in heaven's name is that smell?'

Jeff seemed surprised by the question. Then he leaned over and started to pull off his boots. He pulled off his socks and produced two pieces of rancid meat.

'Steak,' Jeff said. 'It helps the fever. But I guess you already know that.'

The two bits of meat seemed to squirm and writhe in their owner's outstretched palms, grey-green in colour and sweating like living things.

'Who told you to do that?'

'The Gunner. He's a top bloke to have around when you're crook.'

I took a deep breath. 'Get them out of here.'

'Doc?'

'Throw them out of the window if you like. But get those damned things out of this room.'

'But the Gunner reckons you gotta wear 'em for at least three days before they start to work. I've only had 'em for a day and a half.'

'Get them out!'

Jeff was unable to understand my irritation. Neither was Sandy, who had secreted a raw onion in his underpants – at the Gunner's behest – in an attempt to cure scabies, and a ringer called Jonesie reacted with some surprise when I informed him that inserting a stick of celery in his rectum was not an accepted cure for haemorrhoids.

After the clinic I made my way to the stockman's kitchens to remonstrate with the Gunner. I was convinced that he must be entertaining himself at the expense of his more gullible workmates.

But the Gunner had no time for frivolity. He assured me he was a devout and God-fearing man who was doing God's work, and would not be persuaded from the efficacy of his own remedies.

He was a tiny barrel of a man, his body covered with a matt of thick black, curly hair that seemed to burst from the collar of his shirt and right along his arms down to the first knuckle. His face was covered in a blue-black stubble and more hair erupted from his ears and nostrils. The only part of the Gunner that was not camouflaged with this sable coat was his head, which was baby-pale and egg-smooth, surrounded by a fluffy tonsure of hair that clung to his scalp just above the ears.

'God created a cure for every disease in the natural plants and herbs that He gave us, in His wisdom. You can't tell me your drugs are any more powerful than the Good Lord's works.' The Gunner made this speech deep in the bowels of his own kitchen, brandishing a knife in one hand and a partly peeled potato in the other.

'I have no quarrel with the Good Lord,' I told him. 'I just don't see why He would be so unreasonable as to expect a grown man to stick celery up his backside.'

'It's not easy to get celery, you know. Costs a fortune to get hold of the fresh stuff.'

'That isn't the point.'

'Physician, heal thyself!'

'I beg your pardon?'

'It's a saying. It means that there's more things in Heaven and Earth than are dreamed of in your philosophy.'

I shook my head. I didn't seem to be getting through. 'You've got to stop handing out these preposterous remedies. You could do someone some serious harm.'

The Gunner threw the last potato in a simmering pan. 'Professional jealousy, that's all it is,' he muttered, and he turned his back on me and went out the back door, slamming it behind him.

Jealousy was in abundant supply that morning. But I found my second experience of it that morning much more pleasant. I had been curious how Megan would react to her first glimpse of Nurse Jane Goodluck. I had been disappointed that she hadn't been on hand when we first arrived. She finally appeared just as we were getting ready to leave.

I wish I could have captured the expression on Megan's face and had it cast in bronze. I could have hung it on my wall and gazed at it whenever I felt my spirits droop, and it would have revived me. Now all I have is the memory.

When Megan entered the kitchen her face was smeared with sweat and dust. There was a jagged tear in the knee of her jeans and she was limping. My heart leaped at the sight of her, but I tried not to let it show.

'Hello, Megan,' I said cheerfully.

'Hello, Mike,' she said. But she wasn't looking at me. She was staring at Jane, absorbing the platinum blonde hair, the neatly pressed uniform and the carefully lacquered nails.

'You're limping,' I said.

'Had a fall, mustering,' she said. Then casually: 'Who's this?'

'This is Nurse Jane Goodluck. She's our new flight sister.'

'Pleased to meet you,' Megan said, but she wasn't at all. They shook hands.

'Hello, Miss Hoagan. I've heard a lot about you.'

'From Mike, I hope?' She turned to me. 'Finished the clinic?'

'Want me to have a look at your ankle?'

'Do I get a private consultation?'

'If you like.'

Jane looked first at me, then at Megan. She stood up. 'I'll go and find Joe. Tell him we're ready to leave.'

After she'd closed the door Megan dropped into the

chair next to me and I helped her pull off her riding boot. 'I must look a mess,' she said.

'Oh, you don't look too bad,' I told her, rubbing it in. 'When did you hurt your ankle?'

'Yesterday.'

'Is it very sore?'

'I'll live.' Her hand stroked back a stray lock of hair. 'She's very pretty.'

'Who?'

'My horse. Who do you think?'

'Oh, you mean Nurse Goodluck?' I smiled. There is nothing a man enjoys more than inspiring jealousy.

'You hadn't noticed?' Megan said.

'She's very well turned out.'

She put her foot on my lap and I started to remove the bandages. 'Nice job. Who did it?'

'Sean. He did basic first aid in Vietnam.'

'Of course.'

She began to chew a nail. I'd never seen her do it before. 'How long has Baby Jane been part of the operation?'

'This is Nurse Goodluck's first flight with us.' I unrolled the bandage and examined the ankle. 'It's a slight sprain. You shouldn't be riding. You need to rest it.'

'Too much work to do.'

'Rest it anyway. Doctor's orders.' I looked up at her. 'You look gorgeous.'

'Don't lie, I've been working in the yards all morning.'

'I mean it.' I began to put a fresh bandage on her foot. 'This is not a working foot, you know.'

'Meaning?'

'There's no corns, no blood blisters. It's a prerequisite for stockmen.'

'Don't start that again.'

'I'm not starting anything. Just stating facts.'

'We've been through this a hundred times. You know I can't leave the station.'

'I know, I know. You've told me.'

'Oh, Mike, what are we going to do?'

'Wish I knew.'

'Why can't life be simple?'

'It is. It's just the people that are complicated.'

I felt her hand stroke my hair. 'I do love you.'

'Sort of.'

'I do.'

'It's okay. I sort of love you too.' I leaned over to kiss her. I watched her close her eyes, as my lips brushed against hers. I felt her hand stroke my cheek.

'I'm sorry.'

'What for?'

'I went out to the yards on purpose. I wanted you to miss me.'

'I do.'

'Do you?'

Suddenly the door burst open. It was Sean. He grinned. 'Sorry, am I intruding?'

'Yes, you are,' I told him.

'Good-o.'

Megan pushed me away and rounded on Sean. 'What is it?'

'Got a problem with the chopper. Afraid she won't be going anywhere for a couple of days till she's fixed.'

'Damn.'

'Want me to radio to Preston for the spare parts?'

'You know you can.'

'Just thought I'd clear it with you first. Right-o. Hot day. Leave the door open, shall I?' And he went outside.

9

The processes of law and order in Preston were strengthened by the arrival of Sergeant Harry Dawson. Dawson was a big man, an ex-professional footballer who had run to fat. He had a stomach that would not have shamed a pregnant sow, and when he walked it rolled and heaved inside his khaki drill shirt, threatening to escape its cotton prison at any moment, like a disembowelment.

Sergeant Dawson was accompanied to Preston by his wife, Beatrice May. Beatrice May was a garrulous woman, a strange, unkempt creature who would impart the most delicate private information to even the most casual acquaintance. For instance, it was soon common knowledge around the town that the town's new police chief suffered from chronic haemorrhoids and showed alarming symptoms of flatulence if he drank more than one bottle of beer, a feat he performed frequently.

I met Sergeant Dawson just three days after his arrival in the town. I was driving back to the Residence from the aerodrome. I was very tired, having just returned from three days of clinics in the East Kimberley. Suddenly I heard someone sounding their horn right behind me. I glanced into the rear-view mirror and saw the familiar blue-painted utility with POLICE written across the bonnet. Dawson was behind the wheel. He flashed his headlights and gesticulated for me to pull over.

What the hell was wrong? I immediately assumed that it was some sort of emergency and Dawson urgently needed a medical specialist.

I pulled over and jumped out of the car. 'What's wrong, officer?'

Dawson eased his bulk out from behind the wheel and stood up. 'Good afternoon, sir.'

'Sergeant Dawson, isn't it?' I said, and held out my hand. 'Doctor Mike Hazzard. What can I do for you?'

Dawson studied the proffered hand with disdain and walked past me. 'This your vehicle?'

'Well, no. It belongs to the Flying Doctor Service.'

'I see.'

'Is something wrong?'

'Did you know your right-hand brake light is non-operational?'

'Is it? I'll get it fixed.'

Dawson reached into the breast pocket of his shirt and produced a book of infringement notices. He took out a biro and started to note down the registration number of my ancient Holden.

'You're – you're not giving me a ticket?' I stammered.

'I'm afraid so, sir.'

'You're joking.'

'A faulty brake light is no laughing matter, sir.'

I couldn't believe it. I had grown accustomed to the easy-going methods of Dawson's predecessor. In the bush, policemen often get to know most of the inhabitants of their district on an informal, and frequently, friendly basis. Major crimes are uncommon and a stern warning is usually enough to rectify minor offences. The most serious problems occur in the vicinity of the hotels, and an overnight stay in the lock-up to sober up is the common remedy. There is a tacit understanding of co-operation between the community and the police. In other words, things are just not done by the book and the previous police sergeant, Dunnett, and his two constables Regan and Clarke, understood this.

It seemed no one had told Harry Dawson. If they did, he hadn't been listening at the time.

'Look, I've already said I'll get it fixed.'

'A registered automobile should always be properly maintained,' Dawson lectured.

I couldn't believe my ears. In the Kimberley, where the rutted roads and omnipresent dust and the annual floods create an environment never envisioned by Henry Ford in his worst nightmares, a roadworthy car is the exception instead of the rule. 'You can't be serious, Sergeant.'

'I beg your pardon, sir?'

'Surely a warning would be enough.'

Dawson looked at me, speculatively. 'Come with me,' he said.

For one bizarre moment I thought he was about to arrest me. I followed him to the police utility in amazement. Grunting, he reached across the front seat of the car and pulled a large hessian-wrapped object towards him. His vast belly drooped onto the seat like an over-full udder. He straightened and carried the object to the bonnet of the Ford. He folded back the covering to reveal a landscape in oils, a crudely painted bush scene of a boab tree with a range of orange cliffs in the middle distance.

'What do you think?'

I was too stunned to speak. I shook my head and shrugged.

'What's the matter? Don't you like it?'

It was obviously important that I said I did. 'Mmm,' I agreed. 'Very nice.'

'A thing of beauty is a joy forever.'

'Couldn't agree more.'

'Yours for five dollars,' he said.

I stared at him, bewildered. 'What?'

'You can have a choice,' he told me. Underneath the first painting was a second; another bush scene, another

85

boab, another mountain range. 'You're getting one hell of a bargain.'

'I don't understand,' I stammered.

'My wife painted them. She's a very talented artist, my wife. Never let it be said that Sergeant Harry Dawson looks unkindly upon anyone with a love of fine art.' He winked and tapped the infringement notice with his finger. 'Get my drift?'

'You mean if I buy one of your wife's paintings, you'll forget about my broken brake light?'

'What brake light?' Dawson said, and grinned.

'Certainly not! That's extortion!'

He took a deep breath and replaced the hessian covering over the paintings, in the manner of one removing pearls from the gaze of swine. He threw them on the passenger seat of the utility. 'Sure you won't change your mind, sir?'

'I think it's utterly disgraceful that a member of the police force should use his exalted position for personal gain and profit.'

'I see. In that case, I'll have to point out to you that one of your blinker lights isn't working, either. Can I see your driving licence, sir?'

'It's bloody unbelievable! The man's an absolute lunatic!'

Clyde shrugged and opened another beer. 'Yairs, well, looks like we're stuck with him.'

'Got rocks in his top paddock,' Sam said.

'Roos,' Joe corrected. '*Roos* in his top paddock.'

'Are you sure?' Sam said.

Joe looked at me and raised his eyes to the ceiling. 'I'm sure.'

'He tried to blackmail me. He didn't even try to be subtle about it.' It was two days later and I was still furious. 'We have to do something about him.'

'Settle down,' Clyde said. 'Have another beer.' We

were on the front verandah of the residency bungalow. It was a cool June evening and a spray of stars was flung across the cloudless and moonless velvet canopy of the night.

'Another beer, Sam?' Clyde said.

'No, can't sit here cracking the fat all night. Got to be up early in the morning.'

'Chewing the fat,' Joe corrected. 'Cracking the fat is . . . well, it's what . . . oh, never mind.'

'See you bastards in the morning.' He stood up. 'Better go and python the wife's best friend before I go.' He wandered off round the side of the house.

'What did he say?' Clyde said.

'I've no idea.'

'I don't think he'll ever get a grip of the language,' Joe said.

Sam had settled quickly into his new job and had proved a more than capable pilot. He had also become something of a social success, and his brutal treatment of the Australian vernacular had made him one of the most widely quoted men in town. It also drove Joe and I to despair.

'Yairs, well, talking of getting a grip of the language,' Clyde said, holding up the latest edition of the *Preston Bugle*, 'seen today's edition of the Three Minute Silence?'

Clyde threw me a copy of Ryan's newspaper. I took it and held it under the hurricane lamp that hissed and spluttered from one of the wooden beams. 'IS IT A FAIR COP??!!' the headline blazed.

'Seems Ryan's taken up the popular debate,' Clyde said.

'Something's got to be done about the man.'

'Yairs, well, maybe he just needs some time to settle in.'

'What do you reckon, Joe?' Joe was sitting with his elbows resting on his hands, looking gloomily at the ceiling, where the moths and tiny flying insects continued their crazed dance of death around the hurricane lamp. 'Joe?'

'Yeah?'

'What do you think?'

'About what?'

'About Dawson.'

'Oh . . . I dunno,' Joe returned to his reverie.

'No use trying to get any intelligent conversation out of him,' Clyde said. 'He's been moping around like a lovesick bull all week.'

The image was strangely appropriate. 'Yeah, what *is* wrong with you, Joe?'

'Nothing.'

'It's no good, Mike. I've tried talking to him. Let him be miserable. He's happier that way.'

Joe had always been prone to fits of depression and mild paranoia. But it wasn't like him to be so sullen and uncommunicative. He rarely kept his sorrows to himself. He normally relished the opportunity to complain.

'Come on, Joe. If something's worrying you, you know you can talk to us.'

'I'm okay, okay?'

'Come off it, Joe. We know there's something wrong. You're not your usual, unhappy self.'

'Gawd, can't a bloke get any peace?' Joe jumped to his feet and thrust his hands truculently into his pockets. 'I'm going for a walk.'

We watched him disappear down the darkened street. '*What on earth's biting him?*'

'Yairs, well,' Clyde drawled. 'If I didn't know better, I'd swear it was woman trouble.'

The phone on the bedside table clammered to life. I awoke instantly, sitting bolt upright and grabbing it from its cradle in one practised movement. I looked at my alarm clock. Six o'clock. It had to be an emergency. 'Clyde?'

'No, it's Joe. Are you awake?'

My head sank back into the pillow. 'Well, I am now. What's the trouble?'

'Can I see you?'

My mind was still fogged with sleep. 'See me?'

'I have to talk to you. It's important.'

I felt my fingers tighten around the phone. I wished it was Joe's neck I was holding. 'Do you know what time it is?'

'It's light.'

'It's six o'clock.'

'Who cares? I haven't slept all night,' Joe said, his voice dripping with his own misery. 'Can I come round?'

'You might as well. I'm awake now.'

'I thought you must be. You picked the phone up so fast.'

Five minutes later Joe padded up the front path, his woolly mop of ginger hair uncombed, his clothes rumpled, his eyes red-rimmed from lack of sleep. I threw open the door. 'This had better be good.'

'Get out the wrong side of bed?'

I let that one pass. 'You look terrible,' I told him, and led him towards the kitchen. 'What's wrong with you?'

'I wish I knew, I mean, well I do know. But I . . . well, I don't know what to do about it. What would you do?'

'About what?'

'God, Mike, you mean I have to spell it out?'

'You're not making any sense, Joe. Sit down and I'll make us a cup of coffee.' The kettle was boiling on the range. I made two strong black coffees and sat down at the table opposite Joe. 'Now, suppose you start at the beginning.'

'I can't believe this has happened to me.'

'Believe *what* has happened to you?'

Joe took a deep breath. 'Mike, I think I'm in love.'

'In love? You?'

Joe looked hurt. 'Is that so strange?'

'Well . . .'

'I have feelings, you know.' He shook his head. 'I don't know. Sometimes I think you blokes think I'm here just for your entertainment.'

'Joe–'

'This is the real thing. It's driving me crazy. I can't sleep for thinking about her.'

'Who is it? One of the barmaids at the Union?'

Joe frowned with disgust. 'Those floozies!'

'One of the nurses at the hospital?'

'You're getting warm.'

'The little dark-haired receptionist?'

Joe sneered. 'She's got a moustache. I'd rather go out with Adolf Hitler.'

'Well who's the lucky lady, for God's sake?'

'Nurse Goodluck.'

'Nurse Goodluck?' I stifled a groan and gazed into my coffee. Somehow I couldn't imagine our blonde madonna and my bulbous-nosed, gangling pilot as an item.

'Have you . . . does she . . . I mean . . . Joe, you're not serious?'

'Why shouldn't I be serious?'

'It's just that . . . well, I don't know . . . Look, have you told her that . . . how you feel?'

'Christ, no.'

'Why not?'

'That's the problem.'

I shook my head, amazed. 'I had no idea. You hardly ever speak to her. I thought you didn't like her.'

Joe's Adam's apple bobbled in his neck like a rubber ball on a high surf. 'I'm shy.'

I shrugged. 'Well, you'll have to talk to her. I mean, that's part of it, isn't it?'

'Perhaps.' He stared gloomily into his coffee.

'Perhaps?'

'I was wondering if you could help me out.'

I should have stopped it there. I should have tipped the coffees down the sink and thrown him out onto the street. But I didn't. Instead, I said: 'Help you out? How, exactly?'

'I was just hoping you might . . . talk to her for me.'

'*Talk to her?*'

'Just generally. You seem to get on all right with her. I thought you could find out how she feels about me.'

'Find out how she feels about you?'

'Well, you know. You could just bring it up in the conversation.'

'Oh, sure. "*Excuse me, nurse, just thought I'd mention it, our pilot's madly in love with you. Pass the thermometer.*" '

'You don't have to say how *I* feel about *her*. I just want to know how she feels about *me*.'

'You don't ask for much, do you?'

'Please, Mike. I have to know. If she . . . well, if she doesn't think I'm too much of a dill, it'll give me confidence. You just have to talk to her, that's all. Feel out the ground.'

'You make me sound like a sapper.'

'Well, love is like a minefield. Isn't it?'

'Very poetic.'

Joe's face sagged, and his sad eyes pleaded with me to end his misery. He looked like a bloodhound in a dog pound. 'Please, Mike.'

I scratched my head. Something inside me was screaming: *Don't do it!*

'All right,' I said. 'I'll give it a go.'

10

We were on our way to Thalgo. 'How are things out here? Has there been any improvement?'

'Mmm.' Margaret said.

'Mmm yes, or mmm no?'

'It's hard to say.'

'For goodness sake, you sound like a politician.'

Margaret avoided my eyes. 'Perhaps you'd better see for yourself,' she said.

Later that morning I understood her reticence. We conducted the clinic from the tailgate of the Landrover, as usual, and once more there was the usual depressing overload of venereal disease and pregnancies in an already impoverished and overcrowded community. When we had finished, I left Margaret to finish packing away the medical kit.

'I'm going to have a word with Billy,' I told her.

'I don't think it's going to do any good,' she said.

'I have to do something.'

'They just don't understand, Mike.'

'I'll talk to him anyway.'

I found Billy Jajaruru squatting on the ground outside the derelict caravan that served as his home. There was a small fire burning at his feet, and the grey smoke spiralled up through the overhanging branches of an ironbark. A gaggle of potbellied kids whooped and squabbled in the dust around him, their bodies seeming too heavy for the slender stalks of their legs.

As I approached Billy raised his head and gave me a big grin. 'How ya goin', Doc?'

Billy was a loveable old rascal, well past seventy, with a bush of white hair and a thick, curly white beard. He wore his usual uniform; a grey-white vest, ragged brown trousers and an ancient pair of brown leather sandals. He held out his hand and invited me to sit down.

'Hello, Billy,' I said. 'Still chasing your wives round the camp?'

'Not so much these days, Doc,' he cackled.

I squatted on the ground and rested my elbows on my knees. 'How are things?'

He shrugged. 'Orright.'

I took a breath. 'Billy, I don't understand. The last time I was here, I left some medicine. Do you remember. It was a special medicine, it stops your women from having babies if they don't want them.'

Billy nodded his head. 'Yo-i, I remember, Doc. That medicine no good too mus.'

'You mean you've been using them?'

'Sure we use 'em. Mebbe they doan work, I reckon.'

'Of course they work. You can't be using them properly.'

Billy bridled at the inference that he didn't know how to use a good medicine. 'We do just like you said.'

'Then why are all the men and women still getting sick? And there's four more of your girls having babies since the last time I was here.'

Billy shrugged his shoulders. 'I dunno,' he said.

'You must tell your people to use that medicine, Billy. You must tell them.'

Billy doodled in the dirt with a finger, then slowly climbed to his feet. 'I show you. You come with Billy.'

'Where are we going?'

'We bin use that medicine, Doc. Medicine no good.' He shuffled off around the back of the caravan. I followed.

Billy led me into the shade of an ironbark and pointed to the ground. 'We bin make it safe here. None of my boys touch it, I tell you true.'

'Touch what?'

'Medicine, boss.'

I looked down. A long stick protruded from the ground, the thin rubber sheath still unrolled along its length, exactly as I had left it almost two months before.

'Medicine no good to mus,' Billy repeated. 'Missus all time get baby in here.' He patted his stomach to indicate where the troublesome babies were first appearing. 'Mebbe we try another stick, another medicine, more better. Doc? Doc?'

One of the features of life in such a remote community was the need to make your own amusements. There was no organized entertainment, except for the open air cinema that showed grainy and ancient movies every Friday and had the hand-painted disclaimer near the green ticket office: '*If no more than forty of you bludgers show by 8 p.m. the movie's off. All moneys will be refunded and you can all bugger off home.*'

The marshes of the Sound were muddy and infested with crocodiles and sharks so swimming was not an option. The temperature rarely fell below eighty degrees, even in the Dry, so ball games were never popular. Drinking, playing cards and talking were the chief distractions and the greatest enemy for most of the inhabitants of Preston was boredom.

The Eating Competition was the brainchild of Gordon McGlashen, the publican at the Union Hotel. One day Sergeant Dawson boasted to him that he had once eaten fifteen roast potatoes in a minute and a half. Gordon had suggested that there was a man in town who could better the feat, and proposed a competition to prove it. So two days later the town's chief enforcer of law and order found himself sitting at a table in the public bar staring into the steely blue eyes of Percival Stainsforth Renfrew-Ballantyne.

News of the competition had spread quickly around the town and there had been heavy betting on the outcome. Dawson was the logical favourite, but those who knew Ballantyne well had invested heavily on his prodigious talent.

'Yairs, well,' Clyde said, as we took our positions around the table to watch the spectacle, 'I know Dawson's big but Percy's not quite human, if you know what I mean. He's a garbage bin on legs.'

'He'll never better Dawson. It's physically impossible.'

'Want to bet on it?' Clyde asked.

'I already have done.'

Dawson and Ballantyne sat across the table from each other, staring fixedly into each other's eyes, like boxers at a pre-bout weigh-in. Money was still exchanging hands on side bets when Gordon elbowed his way through the mob, a set of bathroom scales tucked under one arm. He stood on a chair and called the gathering to order. 'All reet, shut up and listen,' he boomed. The room fell dramatically quiet.

'What about "Ladies and Gentlemen",' someone suggested from the back of the room.

'I canna see any ladies present and I sure canna see any gentlemen. Except for maybe the two representatives of the Flying Doctor Service,' he added. This was greeted with whistles and catcalls. 'SHUT UP! Guid. Noo then, this here is a challenge match between Sergeant Dawson, on my right, weighing in at' – He shoved Dawson forward onto the scales – 'two hundred and twenty-nine poonds.' Boos and shouts of derision. 'And the challenger, Percy something-or-other Ballantyne, weighing in at . . . one hundred and fifty-two poonds.' Cheers. Percy smiled and performed extravagant acknowledgements to the audience. 'Noo then,' Gordon continued, 'this is the rules. There's nae time limit, and the first man to push his plate away, or chuck up all over the place, loses. I'm the referee and mae decision is final. Anyone who wants to dispute with mae can come outside for a chat after. All reet?'

There were no arguments. Gordon gave the signal and Nellie brought on the first course, lovingly prepared by her own hand that same morning. It arrived, ripe and steaming, on two white enamel bowls. There were groans of horror.

'Okay, tuck in, laddies,' Gordon boomed, grinning. 'Hope ye brought a hearty appetite. Ye'll start with everyone's favourite - boiled liver.'

The two men munched their way through a pound of various offals, five tins of cold spaghetti, half a dozen sticky buns, a beef jerky and damper sandwich, a plate of cold chicken giblets and half a dozen jellied pig's trotters. It was after the pig's trotters that Dawson first started to waver. His jaw slackened and he slumped in his chair. His rate of consumption slowed alarmingly. He struggled to force down the next course, fried calves' brains.

By then it was obvious to everyone that Dawson was a beaten man. It was just a matter of time. Another few minutes and it was all over. It was the boiled crocodile tongue that did it. Ballantyne wolfed down his portion in four mouthfuls, and then glanced over at Dawson's plate, still piled high with the gleaming cream sweetmeat.

He leaned forward. 'I say, old chap, if you don't want all that, can I have it?'

It was enough. Dawson pushed the plate away and stumbled for the door. There was a loud cheer from Ballantyne's backers, silence from the rest. The impossible had happened. David had beaten Goliath. Or, as Clyde put it, 'Raw talent triumphed over cellulite.'

Gordon stepped forward and pushed away the well-wishers, who were feverishly pumping Ballantyne's hand. He put an arm around the tall Englishman and raised a hand for silence. 'We have a winner!' he shouted and held Ballantyne's hand aloft. There was a loud cheer. Even those who had bet against him could not stifle their admiration for his feat. 'May I say on behalf of everyone here,' Gordon continued, 'tha' was the greetest display o' gluttony I have ever witnessed.'

'Why thanks, old boy.'

'Nellie, bring oot the prize.' Nellie appeared from behind the bar with a large, flat brown paper parcel. She handed it to Gordon. He ripped off the wrapping and handed it to Ballantyne. 'This grand painting was kindly donated as the winning prize by Mrs Beatrice May Dawson. An' a bonny looking thing it is too.'

Ballantyne accepted his prize with grace. 'Very kind of you, old chap,' he said.

'And noo, just this once, let me buy ye a drink. On the hoose.'

'I'd love to accept, old chap, but I'd better be getting along,' Ballantyne said, glancing up at the clock on the wall.

'Ye dinna want a drink?' Gordon said.

'Another time, I've got to be getting home now or I'll be late for my tea.'

11

'Doctor Hazzard, you know me, I'm not one to complain, but I'm really in a terrible way.'

'What appears to be the problem, Mrs Foulkes? Over.'

'It's me nerves, doctor. They're shot to pieces.'

'Can you describe your symptoms to me please? Over.'

'My hands just won't stop shakin'. I can't sleep and I can't relax. It's shockin'.'

'How long has this been going on, Mrs Foulkes? Over.'

'Years, I suppose. But I just can't stand it any more.'

'You say you've been experiencing these hand tremors and the insomnia over a long period.'

'Maybe longer.'

'I see. Look, I'll prescribe some sedatives for you. I'll be at the station next week for a clinic. I'll take a proper look at you then.'

As a doctor in a small community I found people telling me things in confidence they would not have dreamed of telling anyone else. They seemed to look on me as a sort of combination father confessor and lonely hearts column. I was eminently unsuited to this role, but no one seemed to realize it. On the occasions that I did profer personal advice, no one seemed to take any notice. Perhaps that was fortunate; they probably just wanted to get their problems off their chest.

Nellie was a case in point. Nellie was the new cook at the Union Hotel, a tall, broad-shouldered girl from a country town in the south-west. She had a round, open face, lank fair hair and a figure that Clyde once generously referred to as 'ample'. Nellie wanted desperately to be liked, and she found eager acceptance in a little town like Preston where the men greatly outnumbered the women.

However, a few months after her arrival, she was saved from her life of sin and debauchery by Ken Ryan. He persuaded her to move in with him, and in return for cooking, washing, and housekeeping, he allowed her to pay half his rent on the rundown weatherboard cottage in Dampier Street.

I knew these details of Nellie's private life because she told me about it. On the days I ventured into the Union Hotel for a proper lunch – tinned spaghetti or tinned curry with tinned rice pudding for dessert – Nellie brought it to my table in the beer garden on a tray and then sat down beside me while I ate it. She then proceeded to pour out her troubles.

'I dunno. Men are funny, ain't they, Doctor?'

'I'll have to take your word for that.'

'When I say "men", I don't mean you, o' course.'

'Thanks.'

She giggled. 'That sounded awful di'n't it? But you know what I mean.'

I nodded, my attention momentarily diverted by a strange lump I had found in the curry. 'Mmm.'

'I mean, I *like* Ken. But sometimes I feel like he's using me up.'

The lump was a piece of petrified spaghetti that had somehow insinuated its way into the curry. I extracted it, and shifted it to the side of my plate. 'What makes you think that?'

'I dunno. He makes me pay half of everything. I reckon I was better off before. Blokes used to buy me things all the time. And I got free board at the hotel.'

'Why don't you move out then?'

'I dunno. D'you think I should.'

'It's not my business really, is it Nellie?' I pushed away the rest of the curry and attacked the rice pudding. It had a skin like a rhino.

'I mean, I do all his cooking for him and everything.'

'Poor sod.'

'Pardon?'

'That's odd.'

'What is?'

'You having to pay half the rent when you do all the cooking.'

Nellie rested her chin on her hand and looked at me thoughtfully. 'So you reckon I should leave him then?'

'As I said, it's none of my business.'

'Percy wants me to come and live with him.'

I took a mouthful of rice pudding. It tasted like wallpaper paste. I couldn't understand it. All she had to do was to take it out of the tin and heat it up in a saucepan. 'I guess you'll have to follow your heart on that one.'

'I suppose you think I'm a bad person.'

I looked into the troubled blue-grey eyes. 'No, Nellie, I don't think you're a bad person at all.'

'Ken says I am.'

'Some people like to see the worst in everything.'

'So you think I ought to leave him?'

I pushed the rice pudding away. It was completely indigestible. 'It's your decision.'

Nellie looked at her hands. She seemed to be making up her mind about something. 'Can you tell me something? I mean, you're a doctor.'

'Is it a medical problem?'

'Sort of.'

'What sort of medical problem?'

Nellie looked around, as if to satisfy herself that no one was listening. 'It's something I promised my Dad.'

I stared at her, confused. 'Go on.'

'Well, what I want to know is, if I stop – you know,

with blokes - how long will it take before I become a virgin again?'

I decided to have another go at the rice pudding. 'This is delicious,' I lied.

But Nellie wasn't about to be put off. 'Well?'

'Why is it important?'

'I gave my word to Dad that I'd be a virgin when I got married. I'm not thinking of getting hitched yet of course, but when I do . . . well I can't lie to my old man, but I'd hate to disappoint him. Do you understand?'

'I think so.' Another lie.

'When I told Ken he just laughed.'

I took a deep breath. 'Three months,' I said.

'Three months?'

'Stay away from men for three months and medically speaking you re-establish your virginity.'

Nellie grinned and got to her feet. 'Thanks, Doctor. That's put my mind at rest.'

I gave her a feeble smile. 'That's all right.'

'I mean, I couldn't tell my Dad something if it wasn't true. He always taught me not to lie about anything.'

'That's right. A person should always be honest.'

She picked up the plate of half-eaten curry and the congealing mass of pudding. 'Enjoy your lunch?'

'It was delicious.'

She leaned towards me. 'Don't tell anyone but I made yours separate. The others just get the glop out of the big saucepans.' And she flounced off in the direction of the kitchen leaving me to ponder the mysteries of truth, love and rice pudding.

12

Below us the patterns of the creeks on the marshes looked like fern leaves. The dark greens of the mangroves bordered the muddy brown waters that fingered into the mudflats from the Sound. As we flew out over open water, the brown shaded into blue. Islands were scattered on the water, emerald on sapphire, surrounded by a halo of dun-pink where the mudbanks surrounding them had been disturbed by the tide.

Sam sat next to me, behind the controls, whistling aimlessly through his teeth. He had settled easily into the job since arriving in the Kimberley. He had proved to be the epitome of icy professionalism behind the controls of an aircraft and I quickly overcame my initial anxiety of flying with a man who had once tried to cripple the *Missouri*. In fact, I had even begun to suspect that he had fabricated the entire story until one day he produced some crinkled and yellowing photographs of a young Japanese in leather flying jacket, posing in front of an ancient single engine fighter on some tropical island. The apple-cheeked grin was unmistakable. It *was* Sam.

'Most people have one life, I got two,' he told me, serious for one rare moment, 'the one before I had the prang, and a new one afterwards.'

I thought that crashing a plane packed with high explosives into the ocean was a little more than just a 'prang' but on that occasion I didn't try to correct him.

Despite his obviously Oriental appearance, he had been utterly westernized. The people of the north-west loved eccentrics, and a Japanese with a Californian accent who attempted to talk like Chips Rafferty was made instantly welcome. Whenever Sam walked into the hotel or the post office or the main store someone would look up and shout 'Banzai, you old bastard!' and Sam would say, 'She'll be oranges,' because now he understood the joke and he would grin along with them. Even Clyde, who had often boasted of his feats against Sam's countrymen in New Guinea, overcame his initial prejudice and developed a grudging fondness for him. It seemed the fondness had deepened to such an extent that he had decided to take him into his confidence.

'Clyde tells me you found a diamond,' Sam said suddenly.

I stared at him, startled. 'He told you that?'

'Sure. You mean it's meant to be a secret?'

'Of course it is.'

'Clyde just said not to tell anyone else. I didn't know I couldn't tell *you*, I figured you must already know.'

This intricate piece of Oriental logic blunted my indignation for the moment. 'Have you told anyone else about this?' I asked him.

'No, I wanted to get to you first.'

'Get to me?'

'Clyde said there were a lot more where they came from, and I figured that seeing as how you're not such a bad sort of a bastard really, you might like to cut me in on the deal.'

'Deal?'

Sam glanced at me, uncertain of his ground now. 'You don't seem to know an awful lot about what's going on.'

'Funny, the same thought has crossed my mind too.'

'See, when I got out of the flying school I still had a few debts. A couple of these little diamonds could solve all my problems. That's why I asked Clyde if I could get in on the partnership. He said I'd have to ask you.'

'Partnership?'

Sam shook his head. 'Gee, Mike, don't you know anything?'

'Doesn't look like it.'

'The partnership between you, Clyde and Gordon to find these diamonds.'

'Look, for a start I don't know anything about any partnership. Second, I didn't find the diamond, it was given to me. Third, I don't intend looking for any others.'

'Mike, it could be worth a fortune,'

'It's the size of a pinhead. I doubt it.'

'Still, better than a poke in the eye with a Bondi tram.'

'Burned stick,' I corrected. 'Look Sam, promise me you won't breathe a word about this to anyone.'

Sam crossed his heart. 'Scout's honour,' he grinned.

I sighed. We both knew very well that there had been no such thing as the Scouts in pre-war Japan. I had a sinking feeling in the pit of my stomach. Something told me that the epilogue to the life of Diamond Jim had not yet been written.

Father Pallemberg was waiting for us at the airstrip in the ancient Land-rover. He was excited.

'You look pleased with yourself, Tom,' I said.

'The Lord has decided to lend a hand.'

'You mean – personally?' Sam asked him.

Father Pallemberg ignored the blasphemy. 'We've found a well on the island,' he told us as he drove back along the track that led to the mangroves. 'It's at the other end of the island, an hour's walk. We have to bring it back to the settlement in buckets. But it's the miracle we needed. With fresh water we can get through the Dry.'

'That's great news, Tom.'

'Yes. Some of the younger men were talking about leaving, but they've changed their minds now.'

'Let's just pray for some kind weather during the Wet.'

'I think we can do it now,' the old priest said, hunched over the wheel, his nose almost pressed against the windscreen.

Sam looked worried. He leaned over the driver's seat and tapped the old priest on the shoulder. 'The track bends to the right up there.'

'Yes, yes, I can see it.' He flicked Sam's hand away impatiently and turned back to me. 'Oh, I think Parrot Island can work, Mike. We just have to find a way to get the turtle and trochus shell to town. We need money to trade with.'

'Slow down a bit,' Sam repeated.

'Am I talking too fast? I always do that when I'm excited.'

'No, you're driving too fast,' Sam said.

'Yes, yes. It's all right,' Father Pallemberg said. 'I've told the elders that they might even be able to set up a canning factory, so that they can sell their fish. I know it sounds crazy, but it might work.'

Sam shook him and pointed straight ahead. 'The road bends to the right.'

'What's wrong with him, Mike. Does he think I'm blind, or something?'

'You are going a little fast.'

'I know this road like the back of my hand.' He pressed his spectacles further up his nose. 'Another three young men came up from Preston last week. Brought their families with them.'

'You sure you can see that bend?' I said.

'Yes, yes. You should see the kids, Mike! How many eight-year-olds are there who know how to build a bark canoe?'

'Slow down!' Sam yelled. 'Watch out for the bend!'

'What bend?'

Until the very last moment I had believed that the old priest really had seen the bend in the track. Too late, I realized that he hadn't been paying any attention to either of us. There was a loud bang as the left front side of the vehicle bounced against a termite mound and sent us careening towards the trunk of a boab. The left-side tyres fought for traction in the soft sand, spinning the Landrover around. Sam was thrown into the front seat on top of me. By some miracle the vehicle stayed upright as we slewed to a sudden stop.

Then just silence. Sam was the first to speak. 'Did we hit the *Missouri?*'

'Missed again, I'm afraid.'

Father Pallemberg jumped out and surveyed the damage with the aggrieved expression of someone who has just had the back of his car dented at traffic lights. He walked around the Land-rover, muttering, examining the damage with shocked disbelief.

Sam and I fell out of the passenger side door.

'I don't understand it,' the priest was saying, 'the road just turned to the right for no apparent reason.'

'I knew it,' Sam cursed. 'I knew you hadn't seen it.'

The priest took off his glasses and rubbed them angrily on his shirt. 'Then why to goodness didn't you say something, young man?'

Sam opened his mouth to protest, but thought better of it. He climbed wearily to his feet and went to the back of the Land-rover to fetch the shovel.

It took us almost three hours to dig the Land-rover out of the sand. By the time I had finished the clinic, it was too late to return to the plane. We decided to spend the night on the island.

The sky shaded from a purple night encrusted with

stars in the east to a violet horizon shot through with burned orange in the west. Night fell suddenly, and a sudden breeze carried with it the taint of the mangroves and the sweet smell of wood smoke.

Father Pallemberg led Sam and I to the group of women and children and old men who sat in a semi-circle around the fire. He sank to his haunches and we crouched down next to him.

'Corroboree,' he whispered.

The songman and the didgeridoo player sat together. The didgeridoo player had one leg tucked beneath him, the other extended, the end of the instrument balanced and supported by the toes of his right foot. The tight knot of muscles around his stomach gleamed with sweat, as they worked to build the supply of breath.

'You used to hear them all the time in Preston,' the priest whispered. 'I remember I used to stand at my back door at nights and yell at them to keep quiet. Now you don't hear them much in the towns. Their spirit is broken. But here they have corroboree all the time.'

It began. The man put the didgeridoo to his lips and began to blow the rich, sonorous bass notes, echoing the ancient heartbeat of Australia's red land. The songman began to beat two boomerangs against each other in a slow circadian rhythm, and sang a long, falsetto note. The effect was timeless, haunting. I felt the small hairs on my neck begin to rise.

The dancers emerged from the darkness beyond the fire, their bodies decorated with ash and ochre. One by one, they entered the firelight with a curious, shuffling movement, the movements of their limbs synchronized to the mournful music of the didgeridoo. They gathered in a circle, their heads to the ground.

'WAHHH!'

Then they threw their heads back, their faces transformed by the performance of their theatre.

'HEEE!'

A resonant intake of a dozen breaths.

'WAHHH!'

Then a wild yell of release, mouths open to the sky.

The men began to dance, quivering their legs at an astonishing rate. They uttered shouts and grunts, losing themselves in the rhythm.

'Not dancing yet,' Father Pallemberg said, 'just playing.'

One of the men moved forward from the group to perform a solo, as the others clapped and swayed in time with the music. He squatted on the ground, uttering a curious croaking sound.

'Frog Dance,' Father Pallemberg whispered.

Next they performed the Kangeroo Dance and then Boy Stealing Mangoes, as they pantomimed shaking a tree and scooping the luscious fruit into their hands. Suddenly one of the men ran forward, shaking his fist, playing the part of the gardener chasing the children from his orchard.

Next was the Bush Fire Dance. The soloist beat at the flames but kept putting his foot in the hot ashes. His howls of pain as he hopped up and down brought screams of laughter from the clapping women gathered around the fire.

After the Bush Fire Dance three of the white-daubed dancers approached the centre of the ring, their bare feet beating the earth. Two of the men circled the other, their spears raised. They began to stab at the air around him, as he ducked and weaved.

'This is one of their great legends,' Father Pallemberg whispered. 'It's one of their great ancestors, a great sea hunter. This is the tale of how he once was caught on the open sea in a storm. Those fellows are the lightning, trying to spear him. The storm sinks his boat, but he swims across reefs and through terrible rip currents to the shore, with his day's catch still intact so that he could share it with his tribe.'

The dancing continued, each an episode in the life of the great sea-hunter, the theatre serving as both an entertainment and a living history of the tribe, as the music of the didgeridoo throbbed and moaned in the background.

After the dance had ended, the men disappeared into the darkness, but the music and chanting and the haunting clack-clack of the sticks continued. Slowly the dancers returned, one leading the others, now without his ceremonial spear.

'This is Martin,' Father Pallemberg told me. 'He's very good. Best dancer I've ever seen.'

Martin stepped out of the shadows, the pads of his feet raised in front of him as he walked, his limbs moving in a slow, exaggerated attitude, as if he was stepping through thick mud. He pantomimed the process of breaking thick jungle, his hand shielded over his eyes as if he was searching for something. Suddenly he straightened, pointing, and the rest of the dancers emerged from the shadows, milling about him.

'What are they doing?' I asked the priest.

'It's called the Dance of the Aeroplane Patrol,' he whispered. 'This is a comparatively new dance. During the war there was a launch that used to travel up and down the coast looking for crashed Allied planes, trying to locate survivors. They used some of the Worora as guides.'

'I suppose I always assumed that the dances dated back hundreds of years.'

'Some of them do. But they're also making up new ones all the time.'

'What dance is he doing now?'

Martin appeared to have his eyes shut. He held his hands in front of him and began to wander blindly in a circle. The children and the women collapsed helplessly with laughter.

'It's not a dance,' Father Pallemberg said frowning, 'it's just Martin's little joke. It's supposed to be me looking for my glasses in the morning.'

The next morning Father Pallemberg took us back to the mainland on the launch. 'We'll come up again in about a month,' I told him.

'Thanks, Mike.'

'I hope things work out for the people here. It won't be easy through the Wet.'

'This country was never easy. These people know it better than anyone.'

'That was before the pension checks.'

The old priest sighed. 'Yes, I know what you're saying. And you're right. Why should they bother?' He fell silent, his eyes squinting against the glare of the white sunlight reflecting on the sea, steering the boat from memory. 'I don't know what will happen to these people. I know a priest shouldn't say things like this, but sometimes I wonder what we westerners have done. We're like a renegade cancer swallowing up every other culture. We consume everything, and absorb nothing.'

I had never seen the old priest so despondent. I didn't know what to say. 'Progress,' I muttered lamely.

'I sometimes think it's quite the reverse. Pointless to worry about it, I suppose. It's like a runaway train. You're on it, but you can't stop it, so you just gaze out the window and wait for the bump at the end.'

'So gloomy, Tom? I should have brought Joe with me. You two would have got on well.'

Father Pallemberg grinned, sheepish. 'I'm sorry. Don't listen to me. I'm just a crazy old priest.'

We fell silent. I watched the cool blue water slip by under the bows and for a moment I saw a turtle finning away from us into the blue depths of the channel. I persuaded myself it was an omen and said a small prayer for the priest and his crazy dreams.

'You and I have to have a talk.'

Clyde looked up surprised. 'G'day, Doc. Want a beer?' It was evening and Clyde was settled into his cane chair, watching the sunset.

'No thanks. Where's Mary?'

'Inside, cooking tea. Why?'

'Because I've got a few things to say to you and I don't want to embarrass her with my language.'

'What have I done?'

'Sam was telling me you and Gordon have formed a syndicate to go looking for Diamond Jim's hoard. Apparently I'm a silent partner.'

Clyde shifted uncomfortably in his chair. 'Yairs, well, I've been meaning to have a chat with you about that.'

'I'm all ears.'

'There's no law against a little free enterprise, is there? Gordon and I are committed to donating a share of all proceeds to the Flying Doctor fund.'

'You can drill for oil in the main street for all I care. But why the hell have you been blabbing to everyone about that diamond?'

'I only told Gordon.'

'And Sam.'

'I didn't actually tell Sam about it. It was just that he was with me when I told Gordon.'

'Who else knows about the diamond?'

'No one. I swear it.'

My anger spent itself. I could never stay angry with Clyde for long. I sat down. 'Well at least you've made up my mind for me. I'll have to hand the damned thing in now.'

'Not necessarily. Not many people know about it.'

'I didn't want *anyone* to know about it.'

111

'As long as you've got it hidden in a safe place.' Clyde stared at me. 'Where have you got it, anyway?'

'In a sock in my drawer.'

'Yairs, well, I suppose that's safe enough.'

'Look, Clyde, I want you to promise me you won't tell anyone else about this diamond. Not until I've made up my mind what to do with it.'

'I promise.'

'Not *anyone*, okay?'

Clyde held up two fingers in the traditional boy scout salute. 'Scout's honour.'

13

The wind-sock hung limp against a sky of watery blue. Sam and I sat side by side on the medical kits in the only shade, under the wings of the Cessna. We could see the red roof of Invercargill in the distance, shimmering among the pale yellow grasslands against the grey-blue of the ridge.

'There he is,' I muttered.

The truck's tyres kicked up a plume of dust as it sped across the plain towards us. A few minutes later Gerry Foulkes pulled up in the Nissan.

'Jeez, I'm sorry, fellas,' he shouted. 'Nearly bloody forgot you. The War Office'll chew me ear off when she 'ears about it.'

I only knew Gerry Foulkes from reputation. Gordon McGlashen had known him in the Territory. He told me Gerry had worked for over twenty years on the Queensland cane plantations and at the mines at Mount Isa so that he could buy into his own cattle property. He had taken over at Invercargill just a few weeks before.

'I held out my hand. Hello, Gerry. Mike Hazzard. This is Sam Noriko.'

'Ow ya goin'?'

'G'day, you old bastard,' Sam said.

Gerry blinked. 'Yeah, g'day.'

'What's the War Office?' Sam wanted to know.

'The missus,' Gerry said. 'Yer'll meet 'er a bit later.' He nodded to the truck. 'Anyway, chuck your things in the back and we'll get goin'.'

I got in the front next to Gerry and Sam clambered in the back. Gerry turned round and pointed to a wooden crate. 'You can sit on the box there if you like. There's just some jelly in it.'

'Jelly?'

'Gelignite.' Gerry's face broke into a grin. 'Bet it's the first time you've ever had a ride on a box of dynamite.'

'Actually it isn't,' Sam told him. 'It's the second time.'

Gerry frowned, puzzled. 'What happened the first time?'

'Nothing, fortunately.'

Gerry shook his head, unable to make up his mind whether Sam was a clown or a madman. 'I see,' he said, but he didn't. He probably wouldn't have believed us anyway.

Gerry Foulkes wasn't tall, but he was broad. He had arms like tree stumps and hands the size of dinner plates. He had a mouth full of gold fillings so that when he opened his mouth it was like looking into a mint. He possessed a raucous laugh, the kind of laugh that infects other people, and sets them laughing too. He was big and he was loud, one of those insensitive brutes who offends without ever meaning to.

'So what are ya?' Gerry was asking Sam. 'A Choong?' It was actually an innocent enquiry but I saw Sam stiffen.

'A what?' Sam asked.

'He wants to know if you're Chinese,' I translated.

'Japanese,' Sam said.

'Where from?'

'California.'

Sam frowned and glanced over his shoulder. 'Come off the grass. I know me geography. California's not in Japan. It's in Canada.'

'No, I was born in Japan. Then I went to live in America.'

'So what are ya doin' in Canada.'

Sam gave up. 'I move around a lot.'

We were bouncing across the plain towards the homestead. Red dust poured into the cabin from the seals under the doors. 'What do you think of Australia?' Gerry said.

'It's dry.'

'Yer not wrong. The trees follow me dog around this time of year. You wait till the Wet, but, pisses down like a cow on a flat rock.'

'I must remember that,' Sam said, mentally adding another colloquialism to his expanding arsenal.

'Don't get no snow though. Not like they do where you're from.'

'It doesn't snow in California.'

''Course it do. Seen it at the fillums. There was a bloke in a red coat and a funny sort of hat and Carole Lombard. He was in the Mounties.'

Sam decided to change the subject. He pointed down at the box between his legs. 'This gelignite . . . is this stuff safe?'

'Long as it don't sweat,' Gerry said and he pulled a voluminous white handkerchief out of the pocket of his trousers and mopped the perspiration off his face. 'Bloody 'ot today, ain't it?'

Invercargill was a spartan paradise on the red plain. The garden, sewn with banana palms, pawpaw and citrus shaded the red-roofed homestead. The house was made of local stone, the verandah supported by rough-hewn cypress, overgrown with purple bougainvillaea.

The place seemed deserted. As we got out of the truck a willy-willy raced across the yard, tossing balls of grass high into the air. A flock of galahs settled on one of the water troughs, scooping up the precious water with their beaks.

Sam and I had our hands on the door handles, ready

to leap out, as soon as we reached the yard. Gerry looked puzzled. 'One of you blokes fart?'

'Just putting some space between us and the dynamite,' I said.

'She'll be sweet. I used to work at a big mine at Mount Isa. I know what I'm doin'.'

Molly Foulkes appeared on the verandah. She was a pale, freckled woman, with big hips, rounded shoulders and a tired, haggard face. Her long black hair had been tied behind her back in a long pony tail, but wisps of hair hung around her cheeks, and she continually stroked them away from her face with quick, nervous movements of her hand.

She was accompanied by Eugene, an unlikely name for a boy with flaming red hair and the build of a ten-year-old sumo wrestler.

'This is the Potato Sack,' Gerry said, introducing us to his wife, 'and this is Stupid.' Eugene gave us a sickly smile.

Molly glared at Gerry but he didn't seem to notice. 'Hello, Doctor Hazzard,' she said. 'We talked last week, over the radio.'

'Yes, I remember.'

Something moved from beneath the skirts around her calves. I looked down and found myself staring at one of the ugliest dogs I had ever seen in my life. It was part kelpie, part blue heeler. It had a scar across one side of its face, extending from just below the ear to just above the jaw, and across its left eye, which was missing. Its right ear was also gone, and there was what appeared to be a bullet wound in its right flank. Its tail had been broken in two places and it had lost one of its back legs.

With great effort it limped down the steps of the verandah, leaned against the front right-hand wheel of the truck, raised its stump, and urinated on the tyre. Then it fell over.

'Nice dog,' Sam said to Gerry. 'What's his name?'

'Lucky,' Gerry said.

'Lucky?'

'He was called Roger but after he castrated himself on the barbed wire fence we had to think of another name.' Gerry jumped up into the cab of the truck. 'The boys are all over at the yards. I'll tell 'em you're here.'

And he drove off, leaving us with the Potato Sack and Stupid.

After the clinic Molly invited Sam and I to stay for afternoon tea. We sat down to fresh-baked scones and strawberry jam and a pot of tea in a real china teapot. It was served on a lace tablecloth with cotton napkins, a startling contrast to the beaten earth on the floor and the torn and ragged curtains on the windows. Throughout the meal Gerry kept up a monologue on the price of fuse wire, and the optimum length of wire to use to preserve the delicate balance between economy and survival.

'Yer supposed to use about forty-five centimetres,' he assured me, 'but I reckon twelve's long enough. 'Specially at today's prices. Plenty of time to nick off and throw yourself flat on the ground before she goes.'

'Surely that's a bit like Russian roulette,' I said.

'Nar, don't use any of that commie stuff,' Gerry said. 'Can't trust it.'

'What I mean is, why take that sort of risk with your life? Not over a few cents.'

'No risk,' Gerry said, wiping his mouth with the back of his hand and emitting a low, satisfied belch. 'I know what I'm doin'.'

After he'd gone, I sat down alone with Molly and asked her if she was still having trouble with her 'nerves'.

''Fraid so, Doctor. I think it's getting worse.'

It's only too easy for a doctor to prescribe sedatives

in such cases. At the busy practice I'd run in Sydney, I was often unable to spend much time with individual patients. Now I was able to get to know individuals, and become aquainted with the psychological causes behind the more nebulous ills.

'Anything worrying you at the moment, Molly?'

She shook her head. 'Not that I can think of.'

'This sort of thing can often be caused by some kind of stress.'

'Not got any stress, Doctor.' She looked puzzled. 'You only get stress when you live in a city, don't you?'

The sudden explosion made me start out of my chair. The windows rattled as the shock waves reached them, and seconds later there was the sound of objects crashing down on the tin roof.

'What the hell was that?' I shouted and ran to the window. A pall of dust rose into the air, and the ground was littered with the dismembered limbs of the ancient boab that had stood about a hundred yards from the house. As the dust cleared I saw Gerry rise from his prone position on the ground, brushing himself down with his hat.

I turned to find Molly still sitting bolt upright, staring vacantly at the empty chair where I had been sitting. A droplet of saliva formed on her bottom lip and spilled out onto her lap.

'In fact I've not noticed any stress at all,' she was saying, 'since we've moved to the country.'

'Mrs Foulkes?'

She looked up. 'Oh, sorry. There you are.'

'Are you all right?'

'Yes, fine. Like another cup of tea?' Without waiting for me to reply, she got to her feet and staggered to the kitchen. She brushed against the table on her way past, knocking a teacup onto the floor. She didn't even hear it fall.

*

'Probably overdid it with the jelly that time,' Gerry told me on the way back to the airstrip. 'Only meant to bowl the bloody tree over, not blow the bugger to bits. Still, it did the job. Damned tree was right in the way of me new water tank.'

As we took off back to Preston I made a note in the file as to the suspected cause of Molly Foulkes's nervous exhaustion. I looked at the pen and realized my own hand was shaking. It seemed I had contracted the symptoms myself.

14

A few days later we held a round of clinics at the stations in the north-east. Nurse Jane Goodluck had come along to assist. The last clinic of the day was at Banjo Patterson's station at Coronation Downs. It was uneventful and afterwards one of the ringers drove us back to the airstrip in a Dodge. Joe had stayed out at the strip to service and refuel the Cessna, so I took the opportunity to broach the tender subject of my pilot's passion with Jane.

'Jane, there's something I want to talk to you about.'

She turned to look at me with the piercing violet eyes. 'You're not happy with me?'

'Oh, it's nothing like that.' The Dodge bounced across a pothole and I gasped as the shock jarred my spine. I glared at the driver, a sullen native boy known as Piles. Jane had asked Banjo how he got the nickname. 'Because he's a right pain in the arse, love.'

Piles saw me looking at him and ignored me.

'What is it you wanted to talk to me about,' Jane asked.

I looked away, regretting that I had ever agreed to help Joe out with his personal problems. 'It's kind of . . . personal.'

Jane blushed. 'Oh, I see.'

'Well, you're a very attractive girl,' I stammered.

She lowered her eyes. 'Thank you.'

'And, well, the thing is . . .' Piles was staring at me. I stared back at him, but he was quite unabashed.

'Please don't say any more,' Jane whispered. 'I quite understand.'

I suddenly had the terrible feeling that she didn't understand at all. 'What I'm trying to say is—'

'I've felt the same way too.'

I stared at her, feeling the situation slowly slipping from my control. 'You have?'

She nodded. 'Since I first saw you. But we mustn't. After all, there's Megan.'

'And Joe.' I immediately wished I hadn't said that. She frowned. 'Joe?'

'No, not Joe. Not me and Joe anyway. Of course not.' I took a deep breath. 'Forget I said that.'

Jane suddenly reached across and put her hand on mine. 'You're very sweet. I'm flattered, I really am. But I'm already engaged.'

'Engaged?'

'His name's Brian. He's a wonderful man. Very handsome and very clever. He's in Perth, but we plan to get married next year.'

A flood of relief washed over me. I felt that I had been delivered of the onerous responsibility I had taken on. Yet I also intuitively knew that I must somehow set the record straight. I had to be clear, precise and also take care not to hurt the girl's feelings. 'It's not that *I* find you attractive . . . Well, of course I do . . . I mean, any man would . . . I certainly do . . . And other men would too, of course . . . Now take Joe for instance . . .'

She put a finger to my lips. 'You don't have to explain.' The Dodge became airborne again as Piles drove us through another pothole, and then I saw the Cessna ahead of us. We were back at the airstrip. What should I do? Should I explain everything and risk embarrassing both of us? It was pointless anyway. She was engaged, so Joe had no hope.

I decided to drop the whole thing.

As Jane clambered into the rear of the Cessna Joe

was at my shoulder, tugging at my sleeve. 'Well – did you talk to her?'

'She's engaged,' I told him.

'So?'

'So – what's the point? She belongs to someone else.'

'You gave up? Just like that?'

'What did you want me to do?'

Joe shook his head in disgust. ' "Faint heart never won fair lady." '

'She's going to marry someone else for goodness' sake!'

Joe gave me a pitying look. 'So you just gave up. What sort of a man are you?'

I was too speechless to answer him. By the time I thought of a suitable reply we were back inside the plane. We flew back to Preston in silence, each reflecting on our own perception of what had just happened.

I had the terrible feeling it wasn't going to be the last I heard of this afternoon's incident.

George and I had arranged to camp overnight at Forsyth Gorge. Clyde had once again donated the use of his Land-rover. We planned to leave early in the morning, and return the following afternoon. One of the doctors at Preston Hospital had volunteered to cover for me if there was an emergency. I was looking forward to the expedition, and had promised to bring a barramundi back for Clyde.

'Bin see that Fish-hook in town today, boss,' George muttered at me while I was loading the four-wheel drive.

'Fish-hook . . . I remember him. He used to work on Brookton, didn't he?'

'Yo-i, boss. You got 'im.'

'What's he doing in Preston?'

'He want to go longa Mount Bartlett,' George told me.

'That's on the way to the gorge.'

'That's what I reckon, boss.'

'We could have given him a lift.'

But George had already thought of that. 'Fish-hook be here first thing in the mornin', boss,' he told me and shuffled back inside the house.

Fish-hook was on hand the next morning, but he was not alone. When I looked out of the window the entire Wanumbul tribe appeared to be camped on the Land-rover. Two youths were asleep on the roof rack, and a white-haired old man was curled up on the bonnet. Four more feet protruded from underneath the chassis and Fish-hook himself was perched on the running board, holding a bottle of beer.

I went to the back verandah and shook George awake. 'George, wake up!'

George tried to rouse himself from his sleep. 'What happenin', boss?'

'How many of your mates did you invite along for the trip?'

'What's that, boss?'

'The world and his wife's crawling all over the Land-rover!'

George staggered out to the front verandah, waved a hand in Fish-hook's direction, yawned and scratched his head. 'What all these fella doin', Fish-hook?'

Fish-hook tried to get to his feet, but stumbled back onto the running board. It seemed he was still half-drunk. There was a cut over one of his eyes and there were dried bloodstains on his shirt. I guessed he had spent most of the previous evening at the Union Hotel.

'My brothers,' Fish-hook said, pointing to the two pairs of feet. He pointed to the bodies draped over the roof. 'My father and my uncle.'

I nodded towards the white-haired old man asleep on the bonnet. 'Who's that? Your maiden aunt?'

'My son,' Fish-hook said.

'Gone prematurely grey, has he?'

Fish-hook made another attempt to get to his feet. 'You take us to Bartlett now?'

I turned to George. 'Did you say he could bring all these people?'

George shook his head. 'No, boss. Just Fish-hook.'

I turned back to the young aborigine. 'There's no room for all these people. Just you.'

'These fellas must go longa Bartlett today,' Fish-hook lied. 'George promise you take us.'

I thought about it. From what I remembered of him, Fish-hook wasn't a bad fellow. It bothered me that he was drunk, but I told myself that all the station hands let their hair down when they came into town. I decided I'd help him out. What the hell. This was the Kimberley, after all.

'All right, I'll take you.' I looked at the bottle of Swan lager clutched in his right fist. 'But no grog, okay?'

'Yo-i, boss. No grog.'

We squeezed Fish-hook, one of his brothers and his ancient, white-haired 'son' in the back of the Landrover. The other three squatted on the roof with the spare water cans. All they had with them was a battered brown suitcase, tied with string.

After an hour, we stopped and allowed the three fellows on the roof to swap places with their two friends in the back. As they clambered in the sour taint of alcohol filled the cabin.

'Have you fellas been drinking?'

'Oh no, boss,' one of them said.

'Just water. Plenty dusty up there.'

I looked at George. He muttered something under

his breath and pulled his battered leather stetson further over his eyes. We drove on.

It took another hour to reach Mount Bartlett. The homestead was about a mile from the road, down a narrow track. I pulled the Land-rover to the side of the dirt road, and got out.

'Okay, fellas. Here we are.'

Fish-hook started to clamber off the roof. He lost his grip and fell, landing on his back. He got slowly to his feet and leaned, swaying, against the side of the vehicle. 'This Mount Bartlett,' he slurred. 'You say you take us longa Hastings Downs.'

'Hastings Downs? That's another fifty miles up the track!'

'Bloody whitefeller. You promise us.'

'I promised to take you to Mount Bartlett, as you asked me to. We're here, and this is as far as we're going. We're turning off the track just up there for Forsyth Gorge.'

'You promise you take us longa Hastings,' Fish-hook repeated.

I went to the back of the Land-rover and threw open the door. 'Come on, out.'

Fish-hook's three friends clambered out. I stood on the running board, reached up for the brown suitcase on the roof rack, and pulled. It spilled open and the contents – half a dozen bottles of sherry, most of them empty – smashed in the dirt.

Fish-hook was enraged. 'Bloody whitefeller! Smashed our grog!'

'You told me you weren't going to bring grog,' I said.

'Bloody whitefeller,' Fish-hook repeated. He staggered towards me and swung at me with his fist.

I took a step backwards and Fish-hook fell on his face. My initial reaction was to escape into the Land-rover. I started towards it but found my way blocked by Fish-hook's other two friends, who had climbed down from the roof. They were stupid drunk.

'Out of my way, fellas,' I said, trying to sound a lot braver than I felt. There was no mistaking the intention in their faces.

But they weren't about to be bluffed. One of them swung at me with his fist. I dodged out of the way but his pal managed to clout me around the ear. I stumbled to my knees in the dust. *This is it, Mike*, I thought. *You're for it, now.*

I looked up. Both of the men seemed frozen to the spot. They were looking at something behind my right shoulder.

'Mebbe better you all bugger off now,' I heard a voice say. I turned around. It was George. He was leaning on the bonnet of the Land-rover, holding the .303 rifle we kept in the back. He held it aimed at the two men.

Fish-hook got to his feet and took a step towards George.

George shook his head. 'You stay there, Fish-hook, or I kill you properly. I never miss from here.'

Fish-hook hesitated and for one terrible moment I thought George was going to pull the trigger. It would have been a terrible mistake because the damned thing wasn't loaded.

Fish-hook was drunk, but he wasn't drunk enough to argue with a rifle. He backed away, giving me one last, sour look. 'Bloody whitefeller. You promise us.' he mumbled. He bent down and salvaged a bottle of sherry that somehow remained miraculously unbroken and he and his troop staggered off down the track towards the station.

I sat with my back against the trunk of a cooliebah and watched an egret fishing in the shallows. The incident with Fish-hook had shaken me. I went through it again and again in my mind. For some reason I felt a deep and lingering guilt. Why? Would I have behaved any differently if they *hadn't* been aborigines? Or was I simply making an effort to excuse them because they were?

George was quiet too. He sat by the fire we had made, staring at the water frothing in the blackened billy can.

'Doan you worry 'bout that Fish-hook,' he said finally. 'That proper cheeky fella. No good too mus now.'

I shook my head. 'I don't know, George. I still feel bad about it.'

'Too mus grog.'

'Perhaps.'

He stared into the fire. 'You feel bad, ay?'

'I suppose I do. Somehow I feel like it's my fault.'

George stood up. 'Come on, boss.'

He padded off along the edge of the water, heading up the gorge. Puzzled, I followed him.

We walked for half an hour. The vegetation was plentiful along the gorge. The banks were thick with tomato bush and wild passion-fruit, and silver cadjeput and Leichhardt pine clung to the waterline. The river did not run in winter, and dark, silent pools were interspersed with areas of hot yellow sand. Logs that had been swept downriver during the last Wet hung suspended in the branches of the white gums, reminders of the gorge's awesome power when the monsoons came.

The only sounds were the occasional raucous cries of the Major Mitchells, and the rush of the wind through the trees, like running water. George padded silently ahead, with me at his heels.

George stopped at the head of the gorge. I looked up. The ancient walls towered over us, striped with black and orange. I had the sudden sensation that there was a presence there, watching me. I shivered in the hot sun.

George pointed ahead, through the trees, to the black maw of a cave on the other side of a limpid pool. Martins darted from the mouth, skimming and wheeling low over the water and into the trees.

'The cave, George?'

George nodded. We walked on through the trees and around the pool. As we reached the cave George pointed above his head at the ancient rock paintings. Then he ducked into the purple shadow.

'George?' I waited until my eyes grew accustomed to the sudden darkness.

'Over here, boss.'

I could make out his silhouette now. I walked towards him.

'There,' George whispered.

At first I didn't understand. The bright sun had blinded me to the gloom. Then, gradually, I could make out the white gleam of the bones. There were three skulls; the rest of the bones had long ago been taken by animals. I took a step towards them, but George grabbed my arm and pulled me back.

'No, boss. We doan touch,' he said. He bent down and pointed to one of the skulls. There was a small hole drilled through the forehead. George made a pantomime of a man firing a gun. I nodded my understanding.

'How long?' I whispered.

He shrugged. 'Long time.'

I stared at the skulls for a long time. We were both silent. Finally George tapped my elbow and led me back outside. One side of the gorge was in shadow now. It was getting late. 'Better we go back now,' he whispered. 'Better we doan stay this place too long.'

We followed the wall of the gorge back the way we had come.

I waited until we were among the trees, and could no longer see the cave before I spoke again. 'What was it, George?'

'Blackfeller bones,' he said. 'Dead long time.'

'How many years?'

'Dunno boss. Maybe million.'

Like most aborigines, George did not have a concept of time as we knew it. 'Whose time?' I asked him.

'Maybe that Pigeon time.' Pigeon was a native outlaw who had murdered a policeman near Wanjina Gorge around the turn of the century.

'They were shot? By white men?'

'Yo-i boss.'

We tramped on a while in silence. 'Why did you show them to me?'

'Dunno, boss.'

'You must have had a reason.'

He didn't answer me. He just shrugged and kept walking. We hardly spoke another word that evening and he never mentioned the incident again.

But I thought about the incident later and I knew why George had shown me the bones. It had been an attempt to explain why I felt so bad about the incident with Fish-hook, why George still called me boss and why, after the three years I had spent in the Kimberley I still felt uncomfortable with the aborigines.

The guilts and the prejudice were not originally mine. By being white I had inherited them. But it would take more than good intentions to wash them away.

15

I had never been on friendly terms with Mrs Denison – no one in the town was on friendly terms with her – but after Colonel Sanders escaped under her house she became convinced that I was persecuting her. She would stop people in the street and tell them she had seen me peering through her windows at night. When her cat – a black shorthair imaginatively named Blackie – disappeared, she made a formal complaint to the police, signing a sworn statement to the effect that I had stolen it for use in a Satanic rite. Dawson came round to interview me, and, during the course of our conversation, he implied that it would be inconvenient for me if a copy of the statement were to find its way, anonymously, to the offices of the *Preston Bugle*. Consequently I purchased my first Beatrice May Dawson original, 'Boabs at Sunset'.

After a few months, however, her complaints about my imagined transgressions decreased. Despite this abatement in hostilities, I was nevertheless quite stunned to find one of her freshly baked fruit-cakes on my doorstep one morning, accompanied by a short note, written in a large, untidy scrawl:

'*Dere Mister Flying Dok,*
    Sorrie for all the trubble I've caused you. Let bygones be bygones.
    Hear is a cake I bakked to show you theres no hard feelings.
    Yaws,
    Mary Denison.'

The cake was the perfect antidote to bitterness. I had often stood on my back verandah and savoured the many delicious aromas emanating from her kitchen, and the fruit-cake looked wonderful. I took it right into the kitchen and cut myself a piece. It was moist, golden and crammed with fruit. I licked my lips and had another slice.

The screen door slammed and George shuffled in. 'Yo-i, boss.'

'Hello, George. Want a bit of cake?'

'Too right. Where you get this one?'

'Mrs Denison.'

George shook his head, his eyes open wide. 'That old missus no good too mus,' he mumbled.

'No, she's okay. I suppose she left this as a sort of peace offering. Here have a piece. It's delicious.'

George and I devoured half the cake, and I took the rest over to the Flying Doctor base. Clyde, Mary, Sam and I polished it off. Joe arrived just as we were scooping up the last crumbs. 'Just my luck,' he mumbled, and went out again.

The cake had been presented on a solid silver cake dish. I took the dish home and washed it. That evening I went to Mrs Denison's house to return it, and thank the old lady personally for her magnanimous gesture. I knocked on the door and waited.

The door opened and Mrs Denison peered up at me through her horn-rimmed spectacles, as if peering into a thick fog. When she recognized me, she gasped and took a step back. 'What do you want?' she screeched.

'I've come to return this, Mrs Denison,' I said, holding out the silver cake dish. 'And thank you very much. It was quite delicious.'

I thought she was about to have a seizure. She looked at the plate, then at me, and made a horrible choking sound deep in her throat. She swayed backwards against the wall, her hand clawing ineffectually for the cake stand.

'Mrs Denison? Are you all right?' Thinking she was about to faint, I took a step forwards to grab her arm. She screamed and kicked me in the shins. I gasped in pain, dropped the dish, and clutched at my leg. I hopped back outside.

The pain filled my eyes with tears. When I looked up, Mrs Denison was gone. I turned to hobble away, but then heard another yell behind me. The old woman was coming at me with a broom. 'What in God's name is wrong?' I yelled.

She didn't answer. Instead she brought the broom back over her head and took a swing at me. It missed my head by inches. I fled. She pursued me up the path, wheezing for breath, flailing at the air around her with the broom. She gave up the chase at her front gate, and stood there, panting, cursing me and all my forefathers. I stared at her, open-mouthed.

What was going on?

Ballantyne appeared, almost magically, from behind the frangipani tree in his front yard. 'Anything wrong, old chap?'

'She just went berserk,' I stammered. 'I don't understand.'

'What's the matter with your leg?'

'She kicked me! Then she tried to attack me with the broom!'

'Tch. Strange old duck, isn't she?'

'All I did was give her back her cake dish.'

Ballantyne raised an eyebrow. 'Her cake dish? Not the one that got stolen, old chap?'

'Stolen?'

Ballantyne leaned on his fence, his eyes twinkling with amusement. Mrs Denison continued to scream recriminations at me from the safety of her front gate. 'The way I heard it,' Ballantyne was saying, 'she left a freshly baked cake on her kitchen windowsill to cool off. When she came back it was gone. Poor old dear has been really frantic about it.'

'Oh, God. She thinks it was me that stole it.'

'Well, it would be the logical conclusion.'

I groaned. 'What have I done?'

If I didn't know what I'd done, the front page of the *Preston Bugle* spelled it out for me that Friday. I'd made page one yet again: 'FLYING DOC STEALS PENSIONER'S FOOD'. I threw the paper in the rubbish bin and marched off to the office of the *Bugle* to lodge yet another complaint with Kevin Ryan.

There is a part of everyone's mind called the Too Hard Basket. It's where we put those decisions that we don't want to make, and wait for life to make up our minds for us. The Too Hard Basket was the place where I had dropped the problem of Diamond Jim's unexpected gift. It wasn't long before Life intervened to resolve my moral dilemma, and decide the gem's fate.

I was on one of the most distant properties in my area. It lay almost five hundred miles to the east, near the border with the Territory. I conducted the clinic that day under an acacia tree in the yard of the homestead. It was an unremarkable afternoon, until I reached my last patient, a ringer by the name of Halloran.

He had bruised his ribs after falling from his horse during a muster. I examined him, assured him that nothing was broken, and prescribed a course of painkillers for him.

Afterwards, as he was buttoning his shirt, he suddenly whispered: 'I heard you found one of Diamond Jim's diamonds.'

I stared at him, open-mouthed. 'What?'

'Keep your voice down,' he said, looking around at Joe, who was about a hundred yards away, refuelling the plane from a forty gallon drum. 'We don't want everyone to know.'

'How the hell do you know about that?'

'Bush telegraph,' he said, referring to the inexplicable way that news is transmitted around even the remotest communities.

'Who told you?'

Halloran was affronted. 'I can't tell you that. The bloke who told me swore me to secrecy.'

'Was it Clyde?'

'Clyde who?'

'Our base director.'

'Nar, this bloke's a fencing contractor.'

'Oh, my God.'

'Doc, just between you and me – is it true?'

'Yes, it's true,' I said miserably. 'Now for God's sake leave me alone.'

Halloran left. As an afterthought he turned back to me and touched his index finger to his lips. 'It's all right, your secret's safe with me,' he said. 'I won't tell a soul.'

He didn't need to. I got back to Preston the following Friday. As I climbed out of the plane Bill McCormack rushed up to me and showed me the front page of the *Preston Bugle*.

I stared at the banner headline in horror: 'FLYING DOC FINDS MISSING TREASURE'.

'How did this get out?' Bill was saying. I thought me and Clyde were the only ones who knew about it.'

There was only one thing to do. Clyde was right. There was no excuse for dishonesty; well, not now that everyone knew about it, anyway.

It was steamy hot in Sergeant Dawson's office. The policeman had his feet on his desk with a copy of the *Bugle* draped over his face. A button of his uniform had popped open revealing the white expanse of his belly,

134

bulging over his belt like the blubber of a freshly slaughtered whale. He was snoring.

I coughed once. There was no movement. I slammed my fist on the desk. 'Sergeant Dawson!'

His left hand groped for the newspaper on his face and pulled it away. He was displeased at being woken from his afternoon nap. He opened one eye and snarled, 'What do you want?'

'I've come to surrender a missing diamond.'

Dawson showed a flicker of interest at this point. He removed his feet from the desk and opened the other eye.

'What diamond?'

'It's all over the paper.'

His senses, if you could call them that, were still dulled from sleep. He looked at the newspaper at his feet, slowly reached down, and picked it up. 'Ah.'

'I believe it's part of the consignment that went missing from a Dutch transport plane in 1942.'

'Says here you've had it for three months.'

'I've been too busy to see you before this.'

He slowly raised himself onto his feet and waddled to the counter. 'Where is it?'

I took the sock from my pocket and placed it on the desk. 'It's in there.'

His nose wrinkled in disgust. 'In there?'

'As good a hiding place as any.'

'Have you been wearing this sock recently?'

'Two or three days. Maybe four.'

'With the gem in question still in it?'

I grinned. I had maliciously transferred the tiny stone to a worn pair of socks as a final act of rebellion. 'I didn't have anything else to put it in.'

He picked up a corner of the sock with elaborate caution, as if it was contaminated with some deadly disease. There was a soft clink as the diamond fell out onto the wooden counter. Dawson picked it up and held it up to the light between his finger and thumb, with the expression of one examining an antique vase. 'Yes, that's one of them,' he said at last. 'You leave it with me. I'll see it gets to the proper authorities.'

'I'd appreciate it. Now then – can I have a receipt, please?'

Dawson sniffed. 'A receipt?'

'A receipt.'

'The receipt book isn't here at the moment. I'll drop it round later.'

'Now.'

Dawson sucked his teeth while he considered this absurd request. 'What's the matter? Don't you trust me? I'm a policeman, you know.'

'So was Himmler.'

'Look, Doctor Hubbard–'

'Hazzard. And I'm not going anywhere without a receipt for that diamond.'

Dawson sighed with disappointment. He realized he had no choice. He bent down and grabbed the receipt book from under the desk. He slammed it down on the counter and reached for the pen. 'This is quite unnecessary, you know.'

'Humour me.'

Dawson wrote the receipt. 'Thank you, Sergeant Dawson.' I turned to leave.

'Just one other thing, Doctor.'

'Yes?'

He reached under the counter and produced a picture of a boab tree. 'Want to buy a painting?'

16

The Flying Doctor base was a mile out of town, on the road heading east to Benowra Crossing. One morning, on the way to the base, I saw a grey four-wheel drive Toyota heading into town. It flashed its headlights and a hand waved at me from the driver's window. It was Megan.

I stopped the car and got out. The Land-cruiser had stopped about fifty yards away. I ran towards it.

'Megan!'

'Hi, Mike.' She jumped out and hugged me. We stood in the middle of the road and kissed. There was a blast from the Toyota's horn.

'What the hell's that?'

Sean leaned out of the driver's window. 'Got a kiss for me, Mike?'

I looked down at Megan. 'You brought company.'

'He's shopping for spares for the Cessna. I just came along for the ride.'

'Come on, Megan,' Sean yelled. 'Hurry up. The doctor's a busy man. He's got places to go, lives to save.'

'Why don't you get rid of that idiot?' I hissed.

'He's a damned good pilot.'

'You're so practical.'

'Ignore him. It's you I came to see. When will you be back?'

'Later this afternoon. Got a clinic at Hawkestone. Where are you staying?'

'At the Union.'

I glanced towards Sean. 'Separate rooms, I hope?'

'Sean's got a double to himself. Can't fit his ego into a single.'

I gave a rueful smile. 'I've missed you.'

'I've missed you too.'

I stroked back a lock of her hair. It was always the same. Whenever I saw her. I wondered why I ever let her leave me. 'We have to talk,' I said.

There was another strident blast on the horn. 'Are we holding you up, Mike?' Sean yelled.

'He's got to go,' I muttered.

Megan just grinned. 'I'll see you tonight then,' she said. She ran back to the Toyota, jumped in, and drove off towards town. I waved, and Sean blew me a kiss out the back window.

A warm, sweet-scented evening. We sat in the beer garden of the Union Hotel, under the shade of the poinsettia tree. Green parrots chattered and fought in the branches above us.

'I heard you had a run-in with Fish-hook,' Megan said.

'It wasn't a very pleasant scene. He wanted to beat me up.'

Megan shook her head, ruefully. 'Poor boy. I heard he's drinking a lot of grog.'

'They all do when they come and live in town.'

'He wasn't a bad worker. But I couldn't afford to keep them all on. Not after this new award. I had to keep the best workers.'

'He was going to try his luck at Bartlett.'

Megan shook her head. 'I heard him and his mates got thrown off. Too lazy.'

'He was all right when he worked for you.'

'Why should they work? They can sit around town and the government gives them money to do nothing.'

'Well, I don't have the solution. I don't think anyone does.'

138

'Don't let it get to you. There's not much you can do about it. The government should have left things the way they were.'

I looked away. 'Well, I don't know. I guess someone thought they were doing the right thing.'

Megan looked suddenly defensive. 'The right thing? Getting them kicked off the stations?'

'I suppose someone figured they should get paid for the work they were doing.'

'My grandfather had nothing when he arrived in Australia, Mike.' Her voice was quiet and controlled. It was a sign that she was getting angry. 'Brookton has a lot of Hoagan blood and sweat on it too, remember.'

'The land belonged to them before it belonged to us.'

She looked away. 'You can't change history, Mike. What do you want me to do? Give it all back and walk away? I love the Kimberley too. And I've lived here all my life, same as they have.'

We were silent for a long time. 'Where's Mister Wonderful?' I asked her, finally.

'You and Sean really don't like each other, do you?'

'I can't understand why you keep him on.'

Megan sipped her shandy. 'I don't have to like him. As long as he does his job.'

'I just can't stand the thought of him seeing you every day, when I only see you every three weeks. If I'm lucky.'

'Then why don't you do something about it?'

'And become a station owner's husband? What would I do all day? Stay home and polish the saddles?'

'You'd rather I became the Flying Doctor's wife, wouldn't you? I could stay home and sharpen the scalpels.'

We'd had this conversation before. It always ended in a fight. 'This isn't getting us anywhere,' I said.

'It hasn't so far.'

There were yells and the crash of a table from the

public bar. It was going to be another lively night at the Union. I put my glass on the table and took Megan's hand.

She bit her lip. She looked angry. 'I won't give it up. I can't be the little wife you want.'

'I'm not asking you for that.'

'No, you're too smart. You're hoping I'll surrender to circumstances and leave you blameless.'

I looked away. Maybe she was right. 'You're doing the same thing to me,' I told her.

Her shoulders sagged. 'You're right. This isn't getting us anywhere.'

A fight had started in the public bar. More curses, and someone's head cracked against the red-grimed window. 'Oh, for God's sake.' I took her hand. 'Let's get out of here.'

'Where are we going?'

'My place.'

She finished her drink and stood up. 'I thought you'd never ask.'

The sun had set by the time we reached the white-painted asbestos house. The black silhouette of a solitary jabiru appeared over the marshes. A cloud of mosquitoes whined over our heads.

'Do you have any other girls, Mike?'

'Now what kind of a question is that?'

'A direct one.' She put her arm around me and moved closer. 'It would be okay. I wouldn't mind.'

'Yes, you would.'

'No, I'd understand.'

'You're only saying that because you know there's no competition. Anyway, I don't want any other girls. I want you.' I opened the gate and we walked arm in arm up the verandah steps. We went inside and I took Megan in my arms. 'I love you,' I whispered. 'I don't want to lose you.'

140

She put a finger to my lips. 'Let's not talk any more.' I felt her warm body press closer to me and then her mouth was on mine. She clung to me desperately. 'No more talk. Just love me.'

Then, a woman's voice from the bedroom: 'Is that you, Mikey?'

I froze. I felt Megan stiffen as she pushed herself away from me. 'Who's that?'

'I've no idea.'

'Coo-ee, Mikey!' the voice warbled again.

I dashed into my bedroom and switched on the light. 'Oh, my God.'

'Hello, Mikey. I've been waiting for you.' It was Nellie. She lay naked under the bedclothes, the sheets pulled coquettishly to her chin. She winked at me and patted the bed beside her. 'Coming to bed now?'

'What are you doing here?' I gasped.

'Ooh, you've brought a girl home with you!' Nellie said.

I looked around. Megan was framed in the doorway, her lips set in a thin white line. She looked at the girl, then at me. 'A friend of yours?'

'I hardly know her.'

'I'll leave you to get better acquainted then.' She walked out.

I started to run after her, and stopped. What was the point? There was nothing I could say that wouldn't sound lame and weak. I stood and watched the door slam.

'I'm glad she's gone,' Nellie told me. 'Perce didn't say anything about another girl. I'm not getting into one of those blancmange à trois. I'm a nice girl, I am.'

'Oh, get dressed, you stupid woman,' I hissed and walked out.

I went outside. I found the Great Ballantyne hiding behind the frangipani tree, exactly where I knew he'd be. I understood everything now. The carpet snake hadn't got into my dunny by accident. It had been placed there deliberately. I also realized who had put Mrs Denison's fruit-cake on my front step and written the accompanying note.

'I'll kill him,' I whispered.

Ballantyne saw me coming and tried to dash for the sanctuary of his own house. He was too slow. I rugby tackled him on his own front steps and then straddled his chest, pinning him down with my knees. He made one feeble effort to wriggle free, then surrendered and grinned sheepishly up at me. 'Something wrong, old boy?'

'You bastard.'

'Come on, old chap, where's your sense of humour?'

'I ought to murder you.'

'Remember your hypocritic oath. It was just a joke.'

'The carpet snake was a joke,' I hissed. 'Stealing the old lady's cake was mildly amusing. This is my life you're stuffing around with now.'

Ballantyne squirmed underneath me, a little frightened now. 'Wasn't my idea, old chap. It was that pilot fellow.'

'Sam?'

'No, the one who looks like Errol Flynn. What's his name? Thompson.'

Suddenly the light dawned. 'Sean?'

'Yes, that's the chappie. He paid me ten dollars. I mean, I'm terribly fond of you and all that, but business is business.'

I rolled off of him and sat down on the step. 'Sean! I might have known.'

'He said it would be okay. It was just a bit of a laugh.'

'Ha, ha.'

'Haven't spoiled anything for you, have I?'

Nellie stormed out of my house, and shambled over, straddling the chicken wire fence. Her face was flushed and her lips were set in a grim line. 'What's going on, Perce?'

'Nothing, my sweetness. The course of true love, and all that.'

'You said he fancied me.'

'I stretched the truth a little. It was a harmless prank, that's all. You mustn't take life so seriously.'

But Nellie took life very seriously. She wasn't accustomed to having her abundant affections trifled with. She decided to exact retribution for her humiliation.

Ballantyne didn't even see it coming. Nellie's right hand jerked upwards and smacked into his cheek, snapping his head backwards and sending his false teeth flying out of his mouth and into a clump of begonias.

'Bloody men!' she shrieked at him. Then, her anger spent, she stormed inside, slamming the fly screen door.

Ballantyne groaned and fell sideways.

I strolled over to the flowerbed, picked up Ballantyne's dentures and tossed them back to him. 'I hope that's a lesson to you,' I told him.

'Lesson to me?' he mumbled. 'What do you mean, old chap?'

'Nellie's never going to forgive you for this.'

Ballantyne fumbled his teeth back into his mouth. 'Oh, I don't know,' he said. 'She took it rather well, considering. And I've still got the ten dollars.'

I turned my back to leave, disgusted. 'One day you're going to go too far,' I warned him, 'and you'll get more than just a slap in the face.'

And of course, one day, he did.

17

Clyde was one of the most dedicated men I had ever known. Apart from over twenty years service to the RFDS, he was also an enthusiastic and indefatigable fund raiser. Clyde organized balls, cricket matches and gymkhanas, all to raise much-needed monies for the Service. One morning I arrived at the base to discover he had secured a permit to organize a raffle.

'What are you going to raffle?' I asked him.

'An air-conditioner. A brand new Bonaire. I'm picking it up this afternoon.'

'Where did you get the money?'

'Yairs, well, paid for it out of me own pocket. I'll pay myself back when the money's in, and we'll send the profit to headquarters.'

'Great idea. I should think everyone in town would fall over themselves to get an air-conditioner. Should have no trouble selling the tickets. How much are they?'

'Fifty cents.'

'Very fair. You can put me down for a couple.'

Clyde sniffed and surveyed me over the rim of his new spectacles. 'Yairs, well, I thought you'd say that. I put a couple aside for you.' He pushed two books of tickets towards me.

'What's this?' I asked him.

'A couple of books. That's twenty dollars.' He held out his hand. 'Come on, then. Cough up.'

For a short time Beatrice May Dawson was the most popular artist in the north-west of Australia. Indeed, almost every home in Preston owned a Beatrice May Dawson original. It was the result of possibly one of the most aggressive and ingenious marketing strategies ever employed.

It soon became common knowledge around town that Sergeant Dawson was serving his prisoners pet food. Breakfast at the lock-up consisted of dog biscuits and a little milk, while long-term inmates enjoyed such delicacies as Pal on toast, and fried roo meat with chips. This was not an act of sadism on Dawson's part, merely greed. He received a meal allowance for each prisoner, and by opting for economy he was able to pocket the difference himself. Since those most affected by his culinary graft were those with the least influence in the community, the practice became established. Having thus asserted his right to do just as he pleased, Dawson went on to rewrite the legislature in his own slovenly hand.

My neighbour, the Great Ballantyne, would often be on his way home just as I was on my way to the Base for the morning clinicals. He was invariably unshaven, tousle-haired and sometimes bloodied. Some mornings he had paintings under his arm, paintings of boabs. And sunsets. The situation struck me as odd.

Each day I drove from my home along Dampier Street, past Sergeant Dawson's blue asbestos house next door to the police station. One morning I happened to look out of the car window and was amazed to see Ballantyne busily at work in the garden. Curiosity got the better of me. I pulled over and got out of the car.

'Ballantyne! What the hell are you doing here?'

Ballantyne looked up. 'Hello, old boy,' he said. He was wearing a ragged, bloodstained shirt and his right eye was swollen shut.

'What happened to you?' I said.

'Bit of a donnybrook at the pub last night, old chap. Must have had a bit to drink, I dare say.'

'Well what are you doing here?'

'Community service,' a voice boomed from the verandah. It was Sergeant Dawson. He emerged into the morning sunlight, resplendent in a stained white cotton singlet and knee-length blue shorts. He had neglected to shave.

'Community service?'

'Couldn't pay his fine so he's repaying his debt to society by some honest labour for the betterment of the community. Aren't ya, son?' Dawson slapped Ballantyne on the back. Ballantyne beamed back at him. They seemed to like each other.

'What did he do?'

'Drunkenness and causing an affray,' Dawson recited.

'If he says so,' Ballantyne said. 'I honestly cannot remember.'

It was at that moment that George appeared at the side of the house pushing a wheelbarrow. I gaped in astonishment. 'George!'

'Yo-i, boss.'

'You seem to have a lot of friends from the criminal elements of our society,' Dawson said.

'So do you,' I told him.

'Crime is my business.'

'I heard that rumour too,' I turned back to George. 'What are you doing here?'

George shrugged, resigned to his fate. 'Gardenin', boss.'

'Why?'

''Moonity service.'

'What did you do?'

George looked at Dawson and then at me. 'Doan remember.'

I turned to Dawson. He had lifted up his vest and was scratching his bare belly like an ape in the sun. 'Why did you arrest this man?'

'He was drunk and disturbing the peace.'

146

'George doesn't drink.'

Dawson shrugged. "Course he does. He's an abo.' Then he added, with his own inimitable charm. 'Seagulls shit, don't they?'

'George, were you drinking last night?'

'It doan matter, boss, I doan mind.'

'Well I do.'

'Troublemaker, eh?' Dawson said.

'I want to know why you arrested this man.'

'Only doing my duty,' Dawson sighed. 'There was some blacks making trouble outside the pub.'

'George was one of them?'

Dawson came to the fence until his face was a few inches from mine. He smelt like a bear's cage. 'Nar, but he's black, isn't he?'

This logic seemed irrefutable to Dawson. I stared at him, aghast. 'You're disgusting.'

Dawson straightened, thrusting out his chins. 'I'm warning you, Doctor Hubbard, that is no way to address a police officer.'

'It's Hazzard, not Hubbard.'

'If you say so.'

'How much is the fine?'

'It doan matter, boss,' George repeated.

'How much?'

'Two "Boabs at Sunset".'

'What?'

'It should be three, but I'll go easy on him for a first offence.'

I reached into my pocket and pulled out a note. I handed it to Dawson. 'Here. Come on, George.'

George put down the wheelbarrow and padded towards me. He stepped over the fence and got into the car. Dawson dashed inside and reappeared with the two paintings. 'Don't forget these!'

I took them from him, opened the boot and threw them in. 'I'm reporting you to the Commissioner of

Police!' I got behind the wheel and slammed the door. Before I could start the engine a shadow fell across the sun and Dawson leaned in through the window.

'One of your tyres is bald.'

'What are you talking about?'

'Your right front tyre. It has insufficient tread.'

'You're joking.' I looked into the pink, fleshy face. He wasn't joking. I groaned. 'How much?'

'Seeing as it's a first offence, Doctor Hubbard . . . Let's see . . . My wife's doing self-portraits now . . . Care to come into the gallery and pick one?'

18

The stench was appalling. Art Johnson looked at me with a pleading look in his eyes, and held out a heavily bandaged hand. 'I think it's gangrene, I can't bear to look.'

Art was Megan's head stockman, a big brute of a man with a ginger beard that spread across his chest like a furry table napkin. He had torn his fingers on some rusty barbed wire while he'd been out at one of the bores, almost a week before. Naturally, it was too minor an injury for a man like Johnson to worry about. It was only now, with the constant nagging pain and the alarming smell emanating from the dressings, that he had decided it might be time to allow the doctor to take a look.

I took a pair of scissors and started to cut away the bandages. 'Who dressed this for you?' I asked him.

'The Gunner. He reckons he trained at a big hospital in Sydney. Says they asked him to become a surgeon but he wanted a job outdoors.'

The mention of the Gunner's name alarmed me. It prepared me for the shock I received when I removed the dressings and found Johnson's fingers had been shoved into a raw egg, now putrid after almost a week on the man's hand. The wounds were infected and swollen and the whole hand was a sticky mess of rotting egg and pus. I reeled back, my head swimming. 'My God,' I gasped. 'What the hell is that doing there?'

'The Gunner reckoned it's a bloody cert for fixing up open wounds,' Johnson said. 'Said they use it all the time in the big hospitals in the city.'

'The only time they use eggs in a city hospital is

149

when they feed them to the patients. And even then they have the decency to cook the damned things first!' I turned to Nurse Goodluck, who was staring in horror, a piece of gauze held across her nose with her right hand. 'Can I leave this to you, Jane? I'm going to have a word with the man responsible for this.'

I found the Gunner in the store. When I confronted him, he regarded me with complete disdain. 'Of course the wound was covered with discharge. The egg draws out the poison.'

'That man should have had a tetanus shot immediately. You have no right to delude these men into thinking you can give them adequate treatment out here.'

The Gunner threw a bag of flour over his shoulder and started to march out of the store. I put a hand on his chest and stopped him. 'I'll have to report this to Miss Hoagan.'

'Do as you think fit. The Good Lord put me on this earth to heal people. That's what I intend to do.'

'You're not healing them, you idiot. You're making them worse!'

The Gunner drew himself up to his full height – about five feet four inches – and looked at me down the length of his nose. 'You're just worried that I'm going to put you out of a job'

'I'm worried that you're going to kill someone.'

'You doctors are all so bloody arrogant,' the Gunner said, and he pushed past me and stalked off towards the kitchen.

He left me no choice. I made a point never to interfere in station affairs but this time I knew something had to be done. I found Megan.

'Look, you've got to tell him to cut it out. Someone's going to get very sick.'

'All right, I'll talk to him,' Megan promised.

'He's a madman.'

She obviously felt I was stretching the point. 'Oh, the men don't seem to mind him,' she said.

'It doesn't matter what the men think of him. You have to put a stop to it.'

'Don't worry. If I catch him doing this sort of thing again I'll . . . well, I'll have to let him go, I suppose.' She seemed unusually reticent about it. It wasn't like her. She could be as tough as any yard boss when it came to business.

'I hope you will,' I said.

She looked up at me. She suddenly looked like a mischievous little girl. 'It would be a pity to see him go, though.'

'Why, for God's sake?'

'Well, when I had a touch of flu last week he gave me this drink he'd mixed up. Next morning I felt a million dollars. Wish I knew what he'd put in it, I'd make a fortune.'

That evening I sat in my living room and admired my latest acquisitions. The once bare walls were now a lively splash of orange and browns. I was the proud owner of half a dozen watercolours, 'Boabs at Sunset', 'Boabs at Evening', 'Boabs at Dawn', 'Boabs at Noon', 'Boabs and Kangaroo' and 'Boabs and Kangaroo at Sunset'.

My sudden acquisition of so many pieces of valuable art had begun innocently enough. I had been sitting in my kitchen earlier that afternoon having a cup of tea with George. It had been a quiet day, and I had just returned from the base after the four o'clock evening clinic. There was a rap on the screen door and a dark shadow seemed to fall across the table. I looked up. It was Sergeant Dawson.

'Doctor Hubbard? May I come in?'

'It's Hazzard. What do you want?'

'If I might have a word . . .'

George got up and headed for the front door. 'Mebbe that fella want 'im lawn cut,' he whispered, and left.

I went to the screen door and opened it. 'What can I do for you, Sergeant?'

'Cup of tea wouldn't be unappreciated.'

'What a shame. The pot's empty.'

'Can I come in?'

'No.'

'Thanks.' He squeezed past me and eased his bulk onto one of the wooden chairs. It groaned ominously. 'It's about that diamond.'

'Oh?'

'You say Diamond Jim gave it to you before he died?'

'We've been through this a hundred times.'

Dawson pulled the biscuit jar towards him and helped himself to one of the biscuits Mary Westcott had made for me. He put one in his mouth and took out another. 'Just had a letter from the CIB blokes in Perth,' Dawson said, spraying crumbs on to the table in front of him, 'they want to know why you waited so long to surrender the diamond.'

I felt my face flush with guilt. 'As I said, I was very busy at the time. I left the diamond in my drawer and forgot about it.'

Dawson put another biscuit in his mouth. 'Not very convincing, is it?'

'They've got the damned thing now. What difference does it make?'

'Wasn't a real diamond, it appears.'

'What do you mean, "It wasn't a real diamond"?'

'It was glass. An imitation.' His paw plunged to the wrist into my biscuit jar and emerged clutching another handful of biscuits.

'So?'

'So there is a suspicion being expressed in some quarters that you may have pulled a fast one.'

'I don't understand.'

'Well, you could have used the intervening period to substitute a fake diamond for the real one, couldn't you?' Suddenly there were only two biscuits left.

'That wouldn't have been a very smart thing to do – would it?'

'No, it wouldn't.'

'So it's not very likely that I would have done it.'

Dawson put both biscuits in his mouth and brushed the crumbs off his shirt onto the floor. Then he leaned back and gave a contented sigh. 'That's not for me to say.' He belched. 'Got a glass of water?'

'Why are you here, Sergeant?'

'I've been asked to investigate the matter further, that's all. Of course, I'm sure a lot of unpleasantness and inconvenience can be avoided, provided my report is satisfactory.'

'This is outrageous. I haven't done anything wrong.'

'Of course not. I just have to convince my superiors in Perth. I'll have to . . . paint the right picture, so to speak.'

'I'm sure you'll do your best,' I said.

Dawson frowned. 'I'll try. But I hate writing reports.'

'A man like you wouldn't like to see a miscarriage of justice.'

'Oh, I don't know . . .'

I sighed. It was pointless to resist. Brave fish swim upstream. Smarter ones swim down. 'By the way,' I said, 'I was looking for some paintings to hang in my living room. Would you know where I could buy some?'

'What a coincidence,' Dawson beamed. 'I've got just the thing.'

'He's an out and out crook!'

Clyde leaned back in the old cane chair and regarded me with surprise. 'Yairs, well, live and let live, I suppose.'

'I wouldn't mind betting he switched the diamond himself. That bloke couldn't lie straight in bed.'

'Calm down, Doc. All's well that ends well.'

'It hasn't ended well! Except for Dawson. He's got a small diamond and thirty dollars in cash.'

'You're jumping to conclusions.'

'Am I?'

'It's all done now. Best to forget about it.'

'I don't want to forget about it.'

Clyde patted his stomach and assumed a look of profound wisdom, the sort of expression often associated with a full belly. 'That was a bonzer tea Mary cooked tonight.'

'If we could get rid of Dawson the crime rate in this town would drop by half.'

'Yairs, well,' Clyde drawled, 'you can't actually prove that old Jim gave you a real diamond, now can you? Maybe it was a fake. One last joke, so to speak. He was a bit of a rogue, old Jim.'

'It was a real diamond. I'm sure of it.'

'Maybe it's best to forget all about it.'

'Is that what you think?'

Clyde considered a moment. 'Well everyone else in town reckons it was all a big hoax. I dunno. I'll have to have a word with Gordon. I think perhaps it's too soon to disband the syndicate just yet.' He looked round at me. 'You sure old Jim didn't say anything else before he died?'

'I'm sure.'

'Yairs, pity,' Clyde said. 'Still, like I said, all's well that ends well.' And he started to hum.

19

I was sitting on my verandah, sipping a beer, watching the sky fade from orange to ochre then through violet to purple. The air was alive with parrots, noisily wheeling and swooping back to their roost for the night. I put my feet on the verandah rail, and settled into a dreamy reverie of contentment.

A few minutes later I was interrupted by the throb of a diesel engine. A Land-rover pulled up outside the gate. I looked up and recognized it immediately. It was Clyde.

'G'day, Clyde. Want a beer?'

Clyde shook his head. 'No, thanks. Not now.' He marched up the verandah steps and stood with his thumbs hooked in his belt, shaking his head.

'What's up?' I asked him.

'It's a sad day,' he muttered. 'A bloody sad day.'

'What is it?'

He folded his arms, unfolded them, then thrust his fists into the pockets of his baggy khaki shorts. His jaw was quivering. I had never seen him so angry. 'It's a bloody sad day,' he repeated.

I got up and put an arm round his shoulder. 'Come on, sit down and take it easy. Tell me what's wrong.'

He sat down in one of the wicker chairs. He was on his feet again almost immediately. 'Some bugger stole the air-conditioner.'

'What air-conditioner?'

'For the raffle. I picked it up this arvo from the freight office, then I had to go into town to the post office. I left the 'Rover parked outside for five minutes. When I came out the Bonaire was gone.'

'Oh no.'

'I dunno. Was a time when you could trust the next bloke. You never used to get thievin' like this goin' on. This town's gettin' as bad as . . . as bad as . . .' He struggled for a suitable epithet, some place that was as low in his estimate as anything could possibly be. '. . . as bad as Sydney!'

'Have you reported it to the police?'

He shook his head. 'Told Dawson you mean? What's the bloody point? That bloke couldn't track a bleeding elephant across a virgin snowfield.'

He had a point. But we had to get the air-conditioner back. 'You'll still have to report it, Clyde. You never know.'

'I can't.'

'Why not?'

He looked at me in exasperation. 'Mike, I've sold all the raffle tickets. Once it gets out that the bloody thing's been flogged, every man and his dog'll be round my place wanting their money back.'

'Well, I guess that's all right. We have to give them their money back. Don't we?'

Clyde finally slumped back into the chair. ''Course we do. The thing is, I can't afford it. I paid for the damned thing with my own money. That air-conditioner cost a fortune. What am I going to do?'

'Look Clyde, I've got a few quid in the bank, I can—'

'I don't want your money. It wasn't you lost the rotten thing.'

'You didn't lose it. It was stolen.'

'All the same, I don't want your money. It's my problem.'

'No, it's not. You were doing this for the Service—'

'All the same, I don't want somebody else bailing me out of my own messes.' He looked away. 'But thanks anyway, Mike.'

We sat for a long time in morose silence. I found it

156

hard to believe that someone would have stolen the air-conditioner in broad daylight. It came as a rude shock.

When I had first arrived in Preston I had been amazed by everyone's relaxed attitude to personal property. No one locked their houses. Doors were left wide open day and night. Once, when I had locked my car after parking it in the street Clyde had stared at me in surprise. 'What are you doin'? Got the Crown Jewels in the glove box?' Now it seemed the ugly world of petty larceny had arrived in Preston.

I got up and started to pace the verandah myself, trying to think of a solution to the dilemma. 'You didn't see anyone near the Land-rover when you left it?' I asked.

Clyde shook his head. 'Not a bloody soul around. Even if there was, you wouldn't expect them to lift a great heavy box like that out of the back of your car. The damned thing weighs a ton. Besides, I was parked right outside the cop station. Some people have got the nerve of Saint Nick himself.' He got to his feet. 'I'd better get back to the base. Mary'll have my tea ready.'

'Clyde, I still think you should report this. When we've explained to everyone what happened, they'll understand. They know it's for a good cause. They won't ask for their money back.'

Clyde gave me a pitying look. 'For a doctor, you're a rotten judge of human nature,' he said. He got in the Land-rover and drove away.

I resumed my vigil on the verandah but the beer had lost its flavour for me and the warm night no longer seemed as serene. I sat for a long time thinking and finally resolved to buy up as many of the remaining tickets as I could. I couldn't let Clyde suffer the loss alone.

But it never came to that.

It was a hot morning, about a week later. I arrived

157

to find Clyde already sitting in the radio hut, busily sorting the morning's telegrams. He looked smug.

'All right, Clyde. What have you done?'

'Morning, Doc.'

'Out with it.'

He put the pencil behind his ear, looked up at me and grinned. 'Yairs, well, you might say I've performed a bit of a coop.'

'Coup.'

'Yairs, whatever.'

'Go on.'

He grinned. 'Drew the raffle yesterday.'

'Oh?'

'All legal and above board. It was drawn in the presence of Sergeant Harry Dawson. Winner's being announced in this Friday's *Bugle*.'

'Who is it?'

'Ken Ryan.'

'Ryan won the raffle. What's so good about that?'

I waited for Clyde to tell me the rest, but instead he returned to his work. 'Come on, what happened?'

'Nothing. He was happy as a pig in manure. Said he always wanted an air conditioner. That little office of his is hotter than hell in the summer.'

'But you don't have an air conditioner to give him.'

Clyde shrugged. 'I know that. You know that. But *he* doesn't know that.'

'Well, what did you say to him?'

'I told him there'd been a delay with the manufacturer and it was due up on the plane next Friday. Said I'd deliver it to him then.'

I couldn't see how this helped. 'The air-conditioner won't magically re-appear before next Friday.'

'It doesn't have to. Next Friday I'll go round and tell him it's been stolen off the back of the Land-rover.'

'And then what?'

'Then I'll say I'm very sorry and give him his fifty cents back.'

I stared at Clyde in shocked surprise. Then I sat down and we both burst out laughing.

Ken Ryan didn't see the funny side of it. Enraged, he printed a front page exposé with the banner headline: 'HOT COOLER EVAPORATES IN DRY'.

But by that stage the raffle was already ancient history. No one was unduly concerned about the loss of the prize in a lottery they didn't win, and Ken had, after all, had his investment refunded. Clyde had his financial outlay recouped, and the profits of the raffle were duly forwarded on to Melbourne headquarters.

It was left to me to carry the torch. It still rankled that someone had stolen something off the back of Clyde's Land-rover, and had remained unpunished. Like Clyde, I had little faith in Sergeant Dawson's powers of detection but I knew Constable Regan to be a man of some resource and not a little intelligence. So I decided to report the theft to the police after all, in the hope that Regan might be able to shed some light on the disappearance of the Bonaire.

As I walked into the police station that afternoon I breathed a grateful sigh of relief. It was refreshingly cool inside. Sticky with perspiration I was happy to wait patiently by the counter for Sergeant Dawson to finish his lunch, a ham and salad sandwich the size and thickness of a drain cover.

'Hello, Doctor Hubbard,' Dawson grunted. He was still eating. Pieces of beetroot and chewed ham splattered on the counter in front of him. He casually flicked them away with the palm of his hand.

'Hazzard,' I said.

'Sorry.'

Suddenly I remembered something. I thought back to the last time I had called on Sergeant Dawson at the police station. I recalled an image of Dawson in his shirtsleeves with his shirt open to the third button, and I remembered that it had been at least five degrees hotter inside the police station than in the street. I glanced towards the back window and the brown-painted Bonaire labouring against the hundred-degree heat.

Dawson noticed the direction of my glance. 'Great invention, air-conditioners, eh?'

'Yes,' I said. 'Wonderful.'

'If you can get hold of one, that is. We used to have to sit in here and sweat like old pork before.'

'I remember.'

'Now then, what can I do for you?'

'Nothing,' I told him. 'Nothing at all.' And I turned and walked back outside to the street. It was baking hot in the sun after the blessed cool of the police station.

Sergeant Dawson was right. Air-conditioners were a great invention. If only you could get hold of one.

20

We were flying east for a clinic at Djilbunga. It was morning, and I was conducting the eight o'clock clinic from the cabin of the Cessna, high in the air above the Kimberley.

One of my first customers that morning was Gerry Foulkes. 'Hello, Doc? I got a problem.'

''Morning, Gerry. What can I do for you?'

'It's the missus. She says she's got a sore throat. I dunno, I reckon she is bludgin'.'

'Can you describe the symptoms for me, Gerry? Over.'

'Like I said, it's just this sore throat. Looks a bit red, but that could be all the tomato sauce she had on her tea last night.'

'I doubt it, Gerry. Has she got a fever?'

'Seems all right. Like I say, she could be bludgin'. You know what women are like.'

I heard a sharp intake of breath behind me from Nurse Goodluck. I could imagine scores of women all over the Kimberley crouched by their transceivers, all reacting exactly the same way.

'Can you bring her to the radio, please? Over.'

'No point, Doc. She can't talk.'

'Not at all?'

'Just a funny sort of whisper.'

'Look, I'll prescribe a course of treatment for you. It sounds like a bacterial infection. Can you write this down?'

'Right-o. Got a pen right here.'

I read out the treatment for him. 'If her voice doesn't

161

get any better we have a clinic due at the station next Wednesday. I can take a look at her then.'

There was a long silence. Finally Gerry broadcast back: 'No need to be in such a hurry, Doc. Some time next month will do.'

We were met at the airstrip by an old red Commer with no driver. Or so it seemed.

As the truck pulled up, the door opened and Eugene Foulkes waved at us. 'Hop in. Bus leaves in thirty seconds.'

Joe gave him a sour look. 'Where's your periscope?'

Little Eugene gunned the accelerator. 'Come on, I haven't got all day.'

We loaded the medical kit into the back of the Commer. Joe walked round the front of the truck and opened the driver's door. 'Okay, hop out, sonny. I'll take over now.'

'The old man said I could drive.'

'You'd have to stand on a chair to reach the brake pedal.'

Eugene slammed the door shut again. Joe took his hand away just in time. 'It's my bus!'

'Oh, let him drive if he wants to,' Jane said. 'It's not a four-lane highway.'

'The little twerp will drive us into a tree.'

'If you don't like it, you can walk,' Eugene said.

Joe, perhaps sensing that further argument might remove even more gloss from his somewhat tarnished dignity, decided to capitulate. Nurse Goodluck clambered into the Commer next to Eugene. I got in beside her.

Once again, Joe was relegated to the tray.

He put one foot on the wheel housing and jumped on. At that moment Eugene lifted his foot off the clutch and we took off. There was a loud bang as Joe landed flat on his back on the tray. Eugene grinned over his shoulder and raced back to Invercargill.

When I had finished examining Molly, there was just an hour of daylight left, and Joe had been unenthusiastic about an unnecessary night flight. We had decided to stay on at Invercargill overnight.

'If you're staying on, I'll take you to me favourite fishing hole,' Gerry had said. 'We'll catch us some tea.'

He had waved a hand airily in the direction of Molly and Nurse Goodluck. 'The ladies can stay here and tidy up a bit.'

Half an hour later we were racing across the plain towards a distant range of low hills. It was then that Gerry made his first enquiry after his wife's health.

'So how's the War Office?' he asked.

'She's got a badly ulcerated throat, Gerry. The antibiotics I prescribed don't seem to have helped much. We'll have to try something else.'

Gerry sat behind the wheel of the Commer, a cigarette clamped between his teeth, and the battered leather stetson pulled over his face. His eyes were slitted against the dust.

Joe sat by the window next to me. Eugene sat on his lap. They glared silently at each other in mutual loathing.

'Jeez, well how about it, eh?' he said. My eyes were drawn to the cigarette in his mouth. It moved up and down as he talked, seemingly attached to his bottom lip by saliva. 'I would have bet quids she was just whingin' again. She's a terrible whinger.'

'It's a very painful condition, Gerry.'

'She never used to be like this, Doc. Gettin' sick all the time. I mean. Big, healthy girl when I married 'er. She's been a bit of a disappointment to be honest with ya.'

Gerry turned off the narrow red track and we

163

bounced across the open bush between the mallee trees. There was a low hill right in front of us. We stopped in the shadow of the hill and Gerry turned off the engine.

'This is the place,' Gerry said. We clambered out.

Gerry's fishing hole was almost invisible until you were nearly upon it. Concealed from view by the hill and the trees, the billabong seemed to follow a natural fissure in the rock, about a quarter of a mile long, but no more than fifty yards wide. Paperbark and pandamus palms clung to the water's edge. Gerry led us to a huge slab of limestone that hung out over the pool.

'Ripper spot this,' he said. 'So many fish they have to fight each other for a drink of water.'

'Heard that one before,' Joe said.

'You'll see.' Gerry had brought two sets of tackle along. 'Sorry. You blokes'll have to toss for the other rod.'

Joe shrugged, and sat down to watch. 'I don't mind,' he said, moody now. 'I never catch anything anyway.'

We baited the lines and cast the lures onto the still, pea-green water. It was close to sunset now and the billabong was bathed in a mercury silver glow, the shadows stretching across the water deep and black and solid as ebony. The orange sun began to slip behind the hill.

'This is bloody hopeless,' Gerry said. We had been at the billabong less than five minutes.

'Only ones that are going to get a feed tonight are the mossies,' Joe said miserably. 'I shouldn't have come.'

'Why did you come?' I hissed at him.

'I didn't want to be left alone with Nurse Goodluck,' Joe whispered.

'I thought you liked her?'

'I do. That's why I don't want to be left alone with her. I want to try and retain my air of mystery.'

The conversation was cut short by the sound of a loud splash in the water. I turned back to my lure, hoping to see the welcome commotion of a large barramundi in the water. There was only a series of slowly expanding ripples on the surface.

'Don't throw stones in the bloody water, you useless specimen!' Gerry barked at Eugene. 'You'll frighten all the fish away!'

'What fish?' Eugene said.

'Go and get the emergency tackle, you stupid kid!' Eugene sighed and began to trudge back in the direction of the Commer. 'And hurry up! It'll be dark soon!' Gerry shook his head. 'Dunno what I'm goin' to do with that boy. Useless as his mother.'

He returned his concentration to the lure. The billabong was silent now, except for the distant shriek of a cockatoo in the pandamus palms at the far bank. It seemed the ideal opportunity to broach a subject that had been concerning me for some time. 'Gerry, I'm worried about Molly,' I said.

'She'll be right.'

'She seems to be under a lot of stress.'

'Bull.'

'People don't get ulcers for no reason. Especially a whole nest of them in her throat, like she has. I think the cause is probably psychological.'

This last statement was effective enough to force Gerry to remove the sodden remains of his cigarette from his mouth. 'You mean she's going nuts?'

'No, of course not.'

'You said she was going psychomological.'

'No, I said these ulcers in her throat might have a psychological cause. That's something quite different.'

Gerry fell silent and considered this a moment. He seemed to be preparing himself to make a weighty announcement. Finally he said: 'Wish that boy'd 'urry up with the emergency tackle. It's gettin' dark.'

I wasn't going to allow him to change the subject so easily. 'I think you're a major part of the problem,' I said.

'Me?'

'Well, the explosives you keep around the place. Molly said she found some sticks of gelignite in her oven the other day.'

'Keeps it cool.'

'She almost lit the fire under it.'

'Stupid bloody woman. Could have blown herself up.'

'That's what she was afraid of, too.'

'I told 'er it was there.'

'She said you didn't.'

Gerry looked uncomfortable. With his free hand he pulled a tin of Log Cabin out of his shirt pocket and opened the lid. He took out a pinch of tobacco. Still using just his left hand, he took his cigarette papers from the same pocket and deftly removed one. One-handed, he rolled himself a smoke. The operation took some minutes. Finally, with the thin cigarette safely clamped between his teeth, he returned to the conversation. 'I know what I'm doin' with that stuff. She's no cause to worry.'

'But she does worry.'

'What am I meant to do about it?'

'It might help if you stopped fooling around with explosives.'

'They're a vital part of my job.'

'Gerry, you're running a cattle station not the French Resistance.'

Gerry sighed. 'All right. In future, I'll only use it when absolutely necessary.'

'I think it would make a profound improvement to Molly's health.'

At that moment Eugene returned with the box

containing the emergency tackle. He set it down at Gerry's feet.

'Okay, son. Hold this,' Gerry said, and handed Eugene the rod. Then he bent down, opened the box and took out a hand grenade. I froze for a moment in horror.

'For God's sake, what are you doing?'

'It's all right,' Gerry said. 'I know what I'm doing.'

'It's a hand-grenade!'

'It's quite safe till you take out the pin.' He took out the pin.

'God Almighty.' I dropped my rod and started to run. Joe, with his more sophisticated nose for trouble, was already fifty yards ahead of me.

I turned round in time to see Gerry lob the grenade into the water. He and Eugene stood calmly by the water's edge and watched, hands on hips, as the grenade exploded in the deep, still waters of the pool, shattering the evening calm. A gigantic spout of water blossomed from the billabong. Flocks of cockatoos and fruit bats rose from the trees, shrieking with alarm, and at once the sky above us was dark with the fleeing birds.

I ran back to the water's edge, shaking with anger and fear. 'ARE YOU OUT OF YOUR MIND?'

'What's wrong, Doc?' Gerry said.

'What the hell are you doing?'

Gerry pointed to the box at his feet. There were five more grenades stacked inside it. 'These little pineapples do a bloody good job when the fish ain't bitin'.'

'Where did you get them?'

'Mate of mine sold 'em to me just after the war. Found 'em at an old army camp in Queensland. Yanks must have left 'em behind.'

'You've kept those . . . all these years?'

'Nearly all gone now,' Gerry said sadly. 'Have to use dynamite when they're all used up, I reckon.'

I turned back towards the billabong. I wanted to weep. The surface of the water was littered with the floating bodies of dead fish. There must have been nearly a hundred. Gerry waded in and scooped up two huge barramundi and brought them back to the bank. He held them up, one in each hand, grinning like a child. 'Quite a catch, eh?'

I realized my anger was futile. Gerry was utterly oblivious to his environment. Not a bad man, simply an insensitive one, a child in a man's body. He could no more comprehend the tragedy of needlessly slaughtering so many fish than he could understand how his larrikinism had scarred his wife.

He threw the two massive fish onto the limestone ledge. 'Got a good feed here, eh, Doc?' he grinned at me.

'I'm not hungry,' I said, and walked back through the fading darkness to the truck.

21

The thermometer on the verandah was still hovering around eighty-five degrees when I went to bed. I tossed under the sweat-soaked sheet, in a light and fitful sleep. When the phone rang it seemed I had been asleep less than ten minutes. I turned on the bedside lamp. It was 2 a.m.

I fumbled for the receiver. 'Hello?'

'Doc? It's Clyde.'

'Problems?'

'My colonial silver-plated oath we have.'

'Who is it?'

'Brookton. I'll patch them through.'

I rubbed my hand across my face and waited for my senses to return. I felt dog-tired and irritable. Clyde patched the call through on the land-line.

'Hello, Mike? It's Megan.'

'Yes, I'm here. What's the trouble?'

'I've got an epidemic out here. Some of the men have come down with some sort of sickness. They're vomiting and they've got terrible stomach cramps.'

'How many of them have it?'

'There's Art, Ginger Mick, Rozza, Cyclone, Symo, old Tom and Dog. Art's the worst. He's in terrible pain.'

'What did they have for tea?'

'Stew. Same as the rest.'

'And the other men are okay?'

'They're all fine. I don't understand it.'

Megan was on the verge of panic. I quizzed her further on the men's condition. It sounded like a case of food poisoning. I immediately thought of the

169

Gunner. But if the men had all eaten the same meal, why weren't they all sick?

'I'll be out there as soon as I can. Stand by, Joe will want to talk to you. We'll give you an ETA when we're airborne. Over.'

I dressed quickly. Somehow I knew the Gunner was responsible. I'd warned Megan to get rid of him. I had a feeling he'd really done it this time.

The Gunner sat in his shorts on a stool in the middle of the kitchen. He was sullen and unrepentant. Megan and I stood over him, the light from the single bare bulb reflecting on his bare pink skull. From the bunkhouse came the sound of the moans and cries. It was like being at Gestapo headquarters.

'Okay, now tell us – what did you give them?'

'If you let nature take its course, they'll be okay,' the Gunner muttered, stubborn to the last. 'It's just their systems purging out all the germs.' Megan and two of the men had found the Gunner skulking in one of the store sheds a few minutes before. Under interrogation he had finally confessed to preparing a secret elixir for some of the men who had come to him complaining of headaches and a sore throat.

'If their systems do much more purging they're all going to dehydrate,' I said. 'Now, for the last time, what was in that drink?'

'You just want to find out all my secrets,' he said to me.

'Oh, for God's sake!'

'Just tell us what you gave them!' Megan hissed at him.

The Gunner thrust out his chin in defiance. 'No.'

To my surprise Megan lost her patience and went to grab him by the collar. Except the Gunner wasn't wearing a shirt. So she grabbed a fistful of the thick black hair that covered his chest instead. She shook him, and the Gunner let out a yelp of pain and surprise. 'Tell the doctor what was in that drink or so help me I'm going to get the stock-whip!'

The poor little man gaped at her and realized she was serious. He started to tremble. 'You're hurting me!' he shrieked.

'I'll have you branded and castrated unless you tell me what you gave my stockmen!'

'All right,' the Gunner whimpered. 'But please let go!'

Megan released her hold on the poor man's chest hair. 'I'm listening,' she growled.

'It's – it's called a Fitzroy Cocktail,' the Gunner stammered. 'Two parts river-water, one part lemon essence and a spoonful of Bex.' Bex was the name of a headache powder, similar to Aspirin.

'Is that it?' I said.

'Yes. No.'

'For heaven's sake . . .'

The Gunner shot another terrified look in Megan's direction. 'There's a secret ingredient,' he said.

'What's that?'

He hesitated. Megan suddenly reached out and grabbed him again. She twisted his chest hair another half turn. He yelped and rose two feet from the chair. 'Meths,' he gasped.

'Holy hell. How much?'

'Tip the bottle up and count to five.'

I turned to Megan. 'Better get over to the bunkhouse. At least we know what we're dealing with now.'

The scene in the bunkhouse was appalling. The smell reached me from across the other side of the yard. The men lay tossing and groaning on their bunks, and the floor and beds were splattered with vomit.

Jane was sitting down on the edge of the bunk at the far end of the room. 'This one's the worst,' she said as

I entered. 'He's going into a coma. I've had to use suction on him.' It was Art Johnson, the head stockman.

'We'll get him to hospital straight away. How do the rest of them look?'

'I've given them all emetics, as you said. They don't seem to be as bad.'

'Knowing Art, he probably went back for a second dose. We'll get him into Preston straight away. I'll leave you here to keep an eye on the others. Think you can cope?'

'I think so. But it's going to be a long night.'

I cursed the Gunner all the way back to Preston. I hated night flights and so did Joe. He mumbled dire prophecies of our impending doom until we landed at the aerodrome an hour later.

I didn't think Art was going to make it. His pulse was weak and slow. I imagined the Gunner standing in the dock, haranguing the judge about the efficacy of herbal medicine as he was led away to prison. A pleasant thought, but it wouldn't do Art much good.

'How much longer, Joe?'

'You asked me that five minutes ago,' Joe complained.

'Well, how long?'

'Look, stop worrying. He'll make it. He's got the constitution of a junkyard dog. It's us I'm worried about. God, I hate flying in the dark. Just my luck.'

Joe was right. Art made a full recovery. A week later he was ready to go back to Brookton. 'Banjo' was in town and offered him a lift back to the station in his ute. On the way out of town Art asked him to stop off at the radio base, so that he could say goodbye.

Art gripped my hand and crushed it in a vice-like grip. 'Just wanted to thank you, Doc. They reckon I was in a bad way when you brought me in.'

'Don't just thank me. There was a lot of people lost sleep for you that night. Joe and Jane Goodluck, not to mention Clyde here.'

'Yairs, well, think nothin' of it,' Clyde said, who was always complaining that people never did.

'I'll watch what I drink in future.'

I felt smug. 'Perhaps you'll keep to established medicines from now on,' I told him.

'Guess I'd better.'

'Besides, the Gunner won't be around to poison you any more. Megan kicked him off the station.'

Art looked amazed. 'She didn't, did she?'

'You seem surprised.'

'Seems a bit drastic.'

'A bit drastic? He nearly killed you.'

Art shrugged. 'He made the stuff too strong, that's all. Anyway,' he added, giving me a playful punch on the shoulder, nearly shattering the bone, 'it sure did cure my flu.'

22

Massey Creek was a dusty and depressing little town. Bottles and cans littered the streets. I saw two aboriginal women drinking flagons of sherry under a massive fig tree. Another had passed out, and lay on the pavement with her head cradled on her arm. The invidious effect of alcohol was more pronounced here than in Preston.

The hospital at Massey Creek was a long wooden building, with a green corrugated iron roof and a wide verandah built around it. It was a mile out of town, on the other side of a shallow creek.

'Why's it so far out of town?' Sam asked me, as we sat cramped and sweating in the back of the grey Nissan.

'It's in case there's an epidemic. They like to keep the germs as far away as possible from everyone else.'

'Must be the hottest place this side of the Black Bourke,' Sam said.

'Stump,' I corrected. 'The Black Stump. Bourke's a place in New South Wales.'

'Are you sure?'

There was just one nurse at the hospital. Sister Marjorie Baker was a tall, thick-set woman with wavy cornsilk hair and a huge lantern jaw. Her skin was so marble pale, it appeared to be almost translucent. It amazed me that she somehow managed to keep it so fair in the furnace of the Kimberley sun. She had been at Massey Creek almost three years, and I had begun to sense that the isolation and the burden of responsibility was beginning to take its toll. Her only support was Dolly, a big aboriginal woman who doubled as cook and cleaner, and Bert, an ancient and wizened old man who appeared at the hospital at infrequent intervals to perform odd jobs and generally attempt to maintain the building.

When I had first met her, Sister Baker had possessed an almost emphatic authority, characteristic of a sister fresh from a busy city hospital. But the solitude and overwork had slowly eroded her sense of identity and in the last few months she had become a shadow of her former self. She was ready to go back to the city, but too proud to leave.

'Good to see you, Doctor,' she said. 'New pilot?'

'This is Sam Noriko,' I told her. 'We have two pilots now.'

'How they hangin', old girl?' Sam said, grinning.

Sister Baker blanched. A shudder seemed to pass through her body. 'I'm all right.'

'Sorry,' I whispered to her, pushing Sam ahead of me. 'He's from California.'

There were four patients. There was an aboriginal woman with a new-born baby, a stockman with a broken ankle, a native boy with diarrhoea, and an old woman with a number of chronic complaints, including diabetes and arthritis, who was considered a permanent fixture at the hospital. I checked on their progress – I had spoken to Sister Baker about each of these cases a number of times – and then she led me through to the outpatients' department.

It consisted of one large room with a desk, an examination table and an old dentist's chair in one corner. The room also served as the dispensary and glass cupboards filled with drugs and surgical instruments, lined the walls.

That morning's patients were lined up in the shade of the verandah waiting for me. I could hear the voices and shufflings through the thin slats of the walls. I laid

175

out my medical kit and my file notes and turned to Sister Baker.

'Well, let's make a start, shall we?'

I heard the moaning as soon as Marjorie opened the outside door. It continued as, one after another, my patients trooped in. It would gradually rise to a crescendo, then fade away. A few minutes later, it would begin again. Finally, I could stand it no longer. I stomped out onto the verandah and looked along the line of mainly black faces. 'What's all the noise?'

An enormous flaxen-haired girl sat halfway along the verandah, her pink face flushed and damp with sweat. Her legs were splayed in front of her and she was panting for breath. A young, painfully thin man in the distinctive jeans, shirt and broad-rimmed hat of a stockman squatted beside her, patting her hand.

'She's got a guts-ache, Doc.'

I walked over and looked down at the girl. 'How bad is it?'

'It sort of comes and goes,' the girl gasped. 'Ow, Jeez, I feel crook.'

'You'd better come inside now. I'll have a look at you.'

The young stockman couldn't lift the girl to her feet on her own. I took her other hand and with the assistance of a couple of other men we managed to get her inside the outpatients' room. As soon as we closed the door she shouted to us that she had another pain. She stood stock-still, gripping our arms, then slowly sank to her knees and groaned. 'Ow, me back's gonna break,' she moaned.

I turned to her young companion. 'How long has she been like this?'

'Since yesterday mornin',' he said. 'She said she had a bit of a guts-ache, that's all. It's got real bad. I reckon it's appendicitis.'

176

I thanked him for his diagnosis and knelt down beside the girl. 'What's wrong? Where does it hurt?'

'Oooooh, OOOOOOHHHHHHHH!'

'Where's the pain?'

'OOOOOOHHHHHHHHH!!!'

'It's all right,' Sister Baker said, 'everybody keep calm.'

'OOOOOHHHHH . . . AAAAAHHHHHHHH!!!'

'Where's the pain?'

'Everybody keep calm!'

'We are calm!'

Sister Baker stared at me, then at the girl. 'What's wrong with her?'

'I don't know.'

'Well, keep calm.'

'You have to tell me where the pain is.'

'ShiiiiIIIIITTTTTT!!!!'

'KEEP CALM!'

Finally we lifted the distressed girl up onto her feet and laid her on the examination table. It wasn't easy. She was a big girl, perhaps fifteen or sixteen stone, I guessed. Her pudgy body was slippery with the clammy sweat of pain. She twisted onto her side, drew her knees up to her chest and whimpered.

'She gonna be all right?' the young stockman asked me.

'I don't know yet. We have to find out what's wrong with her first.'

'She mustn't die.'

'Suppose you tell me what happened.'

The boy's name was Billy. He explained that they were both from the nearby Chalk Hill cattle station. He was working there as a stockman, and the girl had a job as a cook. The girl had started to get the pains the previous morning, and they had become much more severe during the night. The next morning he volunteered to bring her to the clinic in the station ute.

'The trip seems to have made her a lot worse,' he said.

The girl's body gradually relaxed. 'It's all right,' she gasped. 'The pain's gone now.'

'Where does it hurt?'

'My back,' she said. 'Feels like it's gonna break.'

'No, no, its your stomach that hurts,' Billy said.

'It's my bloody pain!' the girl shrieked. 'Mind your own bloody business!'

I lifted up her dress and made a quick examination. It was soon obvious to me that the cause of the problem was not her back, or, as her friend had suggested, her appendix. 'You're having a baby,' I told her.

The girl twisted her head round and stared at me in horror. 'Having a *what?*'

'Didn't you know?'

'I can't be.'

'I can assure you, you are. And the birth is quite imminent.'

'I don't want a bloody kid!'

'I'm sorry. There's nothing I can do about it.'

'Oh shit,' Billy said, 'a baby!' He staggered backwards and slumped into a convenient chair. 'I'm gonna be a father.'

The girl started to cry. Sister Baker assumed control of the hand patting from the girl's young friend. 'Now keep calm,' she told her. 'It's nothing to worry about. Just keep calm.'

'A baby,' the girl groaned. 'Oh, Ker-ist!'

'You must have known,' I said.

'How was I supposed to know? I'm not a bloody doctor!'

'She's always been a big girl,' Billy added. 'I guess an extra few pounds just didn't matter to her.'

I donned a pair of gloves and made a proper examination. The baby was breech. We had to get the girl to the hospital.

178

'When did you have your show?' Sister Baker was asking the girl.

'About a month ago. Went to one at Jacko's place.'

'No, no, the show ... it's a mucous plug that you would have passed in your urine that–'

'Oh, God, this is disgusting,' the girl groaned. 'I don't want to pass any bloody mucus! AND I CERTAINLY DON'T WANT TO HAVE NO BABY!'

'Just keep calm.'

'I DON'T WANT TO HAVE A BABY!'

'JUST KEEP CALM!'

I ripped off the rubber gloves and dashed into the radio room. The afternoon galah session was in progress. 'I found this beaut new diet,' a woman was saying. 'It's sort of like a vegetarian dish, only you make it with meat. Tastes much better.'

'I don't like vegetarian, May. Not even when it's got meat in.'

'This is Flying Doctor calling 6VX Preston. I have an emergency. Come in Clyde.'

'Yairs, this is 6VX. Everyone off the air, please. Okay, Doc, standing by.'

'I've got a young girl with a breech presentation. Been in labour twenty hours already from what I can understand. I'm evacuating her immediately. Please ask the hospital to have an ambulance standing by at the aerodrome. Over.'

'Okay, Doc. Will stand by. Over.'

When I got back into the outpatients' room, the young stockman had his elbows on the desk and was crying into a handkerchief. 'I'm so happy,' he said as I came in. He grabbed my hand and shook it. 'Thank you.'

I pulled my hand away. 'What's the girl's name?'

'Désirée. Désirée Simpson. But everyone calls her Dezzo.'

'How old is she?'

'She told me twenty-three. But I reckon she's only eighteen. She lies about her age to try and pull a bigger wage.'

'Is this her first pregnancy?'

The boy bristled. ''Course it is. What do you take her for?'

Dezzo was in the middle of another contraction, 'AAAAAAHHHHHH!!!'

'Keep calm,' Sister Baker was telling her. 'Just keep calm.'

'MAKE ME HAVE THE BABY NOW!!' Dezzo screamed at me.

'I can't. We're going to take you to the hospital.'

'I DON'T WANT TO GO TO THE HOSPITAL. TAKE IT OUT NOW!!'

'It will be all right. We have to get you to the plane.'

'I don't want to go on no plane! JUST TAKE THIS ROTTEN THING OUT!!'

It wasn't the right moment to explain the mysteries of childbirth to Dezzo. I called Sam in from outside and as the contraction ended the four of us helped her out to the Nissan. As soon as we had her in the back seat another contraction began, and Dezzo groaned, drew up her knees and screamed.

'Keep calm,' Sister Baker told her.

'PISS OFF!' Dezzo shrieked.

'JUST KEEP CALM!'

The young stockman leaped in beside Dezzo and started to pat her hand. Dezzo pulled her hand away. 'Ker-ist,' she moaned. 'Just leave me alone. I want to to die.'

'Will you marry me?' Billy said.

'Oooooooooooooooohhhhhhhhhh.'

'What was that?'

'AaaaaaaahhhhhhAAAAAAHHHHnnnn . . .'

'Say you'll marry me.'

'NnnnnNNNNNNNNAAAAAAnnnnnggggg . . .'

Sam jumped behind the wheel of the Nissan. Sister Baker and I squeezed into the back. 'Out,' I said to the young stockman.

'But I'm the father.'

'No, you're not,' the girl moaned.

'What?'

'I said, you're NOT!'

'But Dezzo . . . remember the time we . . .'

'Ow, Ker-ist, I dunno, maybe you are. What does it matter?'

'It does matter! I love you. I want you to marry me!'

'Oh, please piss off . . .'

I opened the door and Billy tumbled out. Sam threw the Nissan into first and we raced back towards the aerodrome, leaving the bewildered young stockman staring after us, desperately clutching his hat.

'WE'LL CALL HIM WILLIAM!' he yelled, and then he was gone, swallowed up by a cloud of ochre dust.

Two hours later Dezzo was in Preston hospital. The doctors performed an immediate Caesarian and Dezzo was delivered of a baby girl. She named her Chantelle. Within a few days everyone in the hospital had christened her Channo.

Sister Baker had a nervous breakdown a few weeks later. One day she could no longer keep calm. I don't suppose it was Dezzo's fault. They sent her back to Sydney where she happily made a full recovery. A few months later she was back on a hospital ward in St Vincent's Hospital.

Before she left I made some discreet enquiries after young Billy. I learned that he was just seventeen years old, and his father was a prosperous Victorian grazier. Billy had left hearth and home to come to the

Kimberley and get experience. I suppose you could say that he found it.

I would like to say that the romance had a happy ending but romance isn't the way of the bush. In real life absence makes the heart grow less fond and Dezzo saw her young beau just once more, before he returned to Victoria for a quieter life on his father's sheep property, crutching sheep and fighting off pesticide salesmen.

Perhaps it was just as well. The baby didn't look like him, and as Dezzo told me on the flight back to Preston when I asked her if young Billy really was the father; "Ow the hell do I know. If you sat on a bull ant's nest, would you know which one of the bastards bit you?'

23

Megan had her private pilot's licence, Sean, as she delighted to tell me, was a good instructor. Her single-engine Cessna landed at Preston aerodrome a few minutes after Sam and I returned from a routine clinic at Hawkestone. I was waiting on the apron when she climbed out of the cockpit of the plane.

'Megan! I didn't know you were coming into town.'

'I like to come up to the Big Smoke occasionally. Got to do a bit of business before the Wet.'

I was about to kiss her but she neatly avoided me. 'How's your girlfriend?'

'Oh, for God's sake. I've explained that.'

'Yes, I remember.'

'Look, there's a movie on in town tonight. *The African Queen*. Want to come?'

'Got a free night?'

She was deliberately needling me. I tried to ignore it. 'Do you want to come or not?'

She put her head to one side, deciding. What a performance. 'All right,' she said. 'I guess so.'

'Come on. I'll give you a lift into town.'

'Thanks, Mike. By the way – do you go to all this trouble for all your girls?'

I let that one pass too. I could afford to be magnanimous. This time Sean was a hundred miles away, at Brookton.

Joe decided to come along with us that night. He enjoyed the pictures. He always related to Peter Lorre.

We were standing in the short queue outside the cinema, under the light of the street lamp. We were waiting for the proprietor of the cinema to return. He was an old man called Bill, with a brown and dessicated face like an Egyptian mummy. He had suddenly disappeared from his ticket booth when he remembered that he had left the film reels at home. He had quickly locked the gates and shambled off into the darkness, leaving his customers fidgeting in the street.

It was then that Jane Goodluck made her appearance. We were twice blessed because she had brought Brian with her. Frankly, Brian was a disappointment. I wasn't sure what I had been expecting. Certainly, something a little more substantial. Jane saw us, smiled a greeting and came over.

'Brian I'd like you to meet Doctor Mike Hazzard. He's the local Flying Doctor. This is Megan Hoagan. She runs a big property about a hundred miles from here. Oh yes, and this is Joe.'

Brian was shorter than Jane, with a wispy brown moustache and eyes that seemed not quite to focus, which gave him the appearance of a rather evasive weasel wilting under extensive cross-examination. He dutifully shook hands but seemed embarrassed to have met us. Bill returned soon afterwards, and as soon as we got inside he steered Jane towards some aisle seats three rows in front of us.

'Just my luck,' Joe grumbled after we had taken our seats on the hard wooden benches. 'I thought I was up against Superman, and I end up losing out to Clark Kent.'

As soon as the picture started Joe took his revenge by lobbing salted peanuts at Brian's head.

'For God's sake,' I hissed at him. 'You're behaving like a juvenile.'

'I don't know what she sees in him.'

I was about to remind Joe that he was no oil painting himself. I decided against it. It would be just rubbing salt into the wound. Or, in this case, salted peanuts.

I settled back to watch the film. I had seen *The African Queen* before. Seven times, in fact. It was Bill's favourite picture and it showed every alternate Friday. People complained, but they never boycotted the sessions. There was, after all, nothing much else to do.

There was just a single projector so that when one of the reels ran out, the lights would go up while Bill changed reels. Usually someone would have to wander up the back and shake him awake in his ticket booth to perform these necessary operations. On this particular evening the film never progressed as far as the first reel change. Humphrey Bogart and Katherine Hepburn had just buried Robert Morley when the projector caught fire. We all sat in awed silence, watching the celluloid melt across the screen. Finally the house lights went up and Bill hobbled in front of the screen and announced, as if the news might surprise us, that the projector had caught fire. He offered to refund some of our money. Not all of it, of course, because we had seen part of the film.

As we shuffled outside Joe was still brooding about his unlikely competitor for Jane Goodluck's affections. 'Look at him. He's practically a dwarf.'

'Forget it, Joe,' Megan told him. 'There's plenty more fish in the sea.'

'Not round here. Just a few greasy mullet.' He stood with his hands in his pockets watching Jane and Brian disappear, hand in hand, into the night. 'I'm going to fix him,' he finally announced.

'Steady on, Joe.'

'I'm not going to let him run off with the girl of my dreams.'

'Just don't go doing anything rash.'

'All's fair in love and war. It's about time my luck changed anyway. After all, you can't lose 'em all. See you tomorrow, eh?'

*

It was a full moon. It hung low in the sky, brilliant and very close, and the myriad stars sparkled like a fistful of diamonds. The rhythm of the cicadas chattered their rhythmic backdrop to the night.

I put my arm around Megan as we walked. 'Nice girl, isn't she?'

'Who?'

'That girl who was there tonight. What's her name? Ginny Fortune?'

'Jane Goodluck.'

'Is she still working with you?'

It appeared to be an innocent enquiry on the face of it but immediately the alarm bells started to ring. 'Yes, she still works with us.'

'Very attractive girl, isn't she?'

'Mmmm.'

'What does that mean?'

'What does what mean?' I asked.

' "Mmmm." It could mean anything.'

'Sean thinks she's attractive too.'

This was the moment I knew he had done for me again. Sean had never given up on his attempts to white-ant my romance with Megan. 'Does he?' I tried to sound as casual as possible.

'He said he asked her out the last time he was in town. She told him she couldn't go because she was already going out with you. Anyway. that's what he said.'

A blatant lie. 'For God's sake, Megan, you know what Sean's up to.'

'Of course I do.. That's why I decided to get it from the horse's mouth. So to speak.'

'You talked to Jane?'

'You sound surprised.'

'Go on.' My mind churned over the memory of my feeble attempt to win her over for Joe. I had the feeling it was about to return to haunt me.

'She was evasive.' *Good girl!* 'Which made me immediately suspicious.' *Oh my God!*

'Megan, darling, you have my word of honour–'

'It's your honour that's in question.'

We had reached the hotel. We stopped outside. I took her hands and looked at her. Her face was set, cold and grim. Or perhaps it was just the light. 'It's early. Coming back to my place?'

'No, Mike. I've been thinking.' *Uh-oh.* 'Maybe we should end it. This isn't going anywhere.'

'I don't want it to end. I love you.'

'He said you'd say that.'

'Who?'

'Sean.'

Sean! 'Megan, please. Let's talk about it.'

She shook her head. 'Talk is all we ever do,' she said, and there was real sadness in her voice. 'Goodbye, Mike.' She turned and walked inside.

Talk is all we ever do. Maybe she was right after all, because I didn't try to stop her.

24

'What did you think of Brian?' Jane asked me.

Joe glared at me from behind the controls of the Cessna. I tried to avoid his eyes. 'Seems like a very nice young chap.'

'I knew you'd both like him. He's studying to be an accountant. He's really smart.'

'Can he fly a plane?' Joe asked.

Jane smiled, and said in the tone of an overly proud mother: 'He got his private pilot's licence last year. Did the studies in his spare time after university.'

Joe looked at his watch. 'Well that's enough talk. Let's get going.'

We stowed the rest of the medical equipment into the back and I clambered into the passenger seat next to Joe. Jane sat behind me. 'He's only up here for the week,' she went on. 'I hope he gets to see a bit of the country.'

'Funny you should say that,' Joe said. 'I was going to suggest you bring him camping with us tomorrow. Me and Mike and Clyde are going off to do a spot of fishing overnight at Channon Gorge.'

'I'm sure he'd love it.'

'Good. That's settled then.' And Joe turned to me and did something very unusual. He grinned.

I didn't like this. I didn't like it at all.

We bounced along in the Land-rover, heading north up the Beef Road towards the gorge. Clyde drove and I sat in the seat beside him, trying to remain aloof from Joe's machinations. He sat in the back with Jane and Brian. Jane, dressed only in faded green slacks and an old blouse, looked stunning. Even for a night in the bush she had remembered to use her eyeliner to accentuate her violet eyes and her hair was washed and neatly plaited.

'Of course you have to be careful in the bush,' Joe was telling Brian. 'There's snakes everywhere. One bite can kill a grown man in ten minutes. They reckon it can be an agonizingly painful way to go. Isn't that right, Mike?'

I didn't answer him. I knew what he was up to.

'Then there's the crocodiles. Twelve, eighteen, sometimes . . . sometimes forty feet long.' A shocking exaggeration. 'Of course they don't kill you straight off. What they do is, they grab you in their jaws and–'

'Please, Joe,' Jane said. She looked suddenly pale.

'It's all right. You're safe with me,' he told her. 'But it's as well that Brian knows about these things. Him being a city slicker and everything.'

Brian nodded and said nothing. Clyde just shook his head and kept his eyes on the endless red road ahead.

Joe was just warming up. He didn't really get started until we reached the gorge.

Clyde had taken Jane and Brian into the bush to show them the clear black pool where we would fish. Joe and I stayed behind at the camp. As soon as the others were out of sight he went to the cabin of the Land-rover and fished something out from beneath the passenger seat. It was a small eskie. He opened it. It was full of live bait.

'What are you going to do with that?'

'You'll see.' He put the eskie down and began to collect some small stones and twigs to start the fire. 'Get hungry when I come camping. Must be all the fresh air.'

'You're up to something.'

'Not me, Mike. Not honest Joe.' As soon as the fire was alight Joe produced the skillet from the back of

189

the Land-rover, added some butter and began to heat the pan over the coals. 'Reckon they'll be long, Mike?'

'Clyde said they'd be back in ten minutes to help us set up the tents.'

'Good-o,' He reached into the plastic bag, grabbed a handful of writhing pink worms, and threw them on the skillet.

'What in heaven's name are you doing?'

'Bush tucker,' Joe said.

'That's fish bait!'

The tiny larvae had begun to pop and crackle on the skillet. Suddenly I heard voices from the trees behind us. It was Clyde and the two young lovers.

'Hey, Brian,' Joe shouted. 'Feel like something to eat?'

Brian sauntered across. He was wearing neat blue shorts and his legs were pink, hairless and rail thin. I felt hopelessly sorry for him. 'Yeah,' Brian said. 'I'm starving.' He looked at the live bait frying on the skillet. 'What are they?'

'Witchetty grubs,' Joe lied. 'Just dug 'em up fresh. I've just had a couple of platefuls. Want to finish them off?' He poured the panful onto an enamel plate and passed it to Brian with a tin fork.

Witchetty grubs are a larvae found in old decayed wood or in vertical burrows under the ground. The aborigines eat them toasted over hot coals and they taste a little like the white of an egg. This was not what Joe had presented to Brian. Live bait are maggots with no nutritional value whatsoever.

Brian examined the contents of his plate suspiciously. 'You sure you can eat these?'

'Try one,' Joe insisted. 'The aborigines reckon they're a delicacy.'

Brian didn't just try one. He scooped up a forkful and shoved them in his mouth. He started to chew.

I looked at Joe. He had his jaw clenched tight, trying

to contain the explosion of pure joy that threatened to escape. I waited for Brian to react to the terrible taste of the maggots that Joe had just duped him into eating.

Brian swallowed. 'Not bad,' he murmured.

'Not bad?' Joe said. The look of eager expectancy on his face began to fade.

'Not bad at all. Bloody good, in fact.' He scooped up another mouthful.

Joe turned away and looked at me. 'Christ, he's not human,' he muttered.

Brian finished the plate and saw the eskie by Joe's foot. 'Jeez, mate, you've caught a bagful,' he shouted. 'Mind if I have some more.'

Joe nodded and wandered off into the bush. He was looking very unwell.

The next day was a scorcher and we went down to the pool to cool off. Jane went back to the Land-rover to slip into her bathing costume, a pink one-piece number that made Joe close his eyes and groan. She ran laughing into the water followed by Brian, still wearing his neat blue denim shorts. His body was pale and bony thin.

'Look at them,' Joe complained. 'It's like Snow White going off with one of the dwarfs. Life just isn't fair.' He stripped off his shirt. His body was pale and bony thin. But he was, at least, a head taller. He ran into the water with them.

'Is it safe to swim here?' Brian shouted.

'Yeah, you don't get saltwater crocs round here,' Joe shouted back, but he was looking at Jane. 'I'll keep a lookout for you, anyway. I've got a nose for crocs. I can smell them a mile off.'

'They smell do they?' Brian said.

'Well most people can't pick it,' Joe told him. 'But if you're an experienced bushman, you get a sort of sixth sense.'

'Oh, I see.'

'Salties are the only ones you've got to worry about. They're killers. Johnson crocs will take a dog, but they won't bother humans.'

To show his disdain for all reptiles, Joe waded in as far as his chest. He began to swim. Brian and Jane still hovered cautiously in the shallows.

'What would you do if you did see a croc though, Joe?' Brian shouted.

'Well the important thing is not to show fear. Animals can always tell when you're afraid. You should just keep calm and get out of the water.'

'Well then,' I heard Brian yell back at him, 'keep calm and get out of the water.'

'What?'

'Keep calm and get out of the water.'

Joe turned. He yelped and seemed to rise out of the water. 'IT'S A BLOODY CROCODILE!' Clyde and I leaped to our feet and watched as Joe splashed and thrashed and stumbled towards the bank. It was almost as if he was walking on the surface of the water. He didn't stop running until he was ten yards past us.

Brian was still up to his knees in the pool. He scooped Jane up in his arms and held her clear of the water. 'It's all right,' he yelled. 'It's only a Johnson!' He turned and calmly made his way back to the bank.

I turned and looked at Joe. 'Strike two for Brian,' I whispered.

'Just my luck,' Joe said. 'A bloody smart-arse.'

Joe must have sensed defeat. Later that afternoon, when Brian strolled into the camp swinging a dead tiger snake, he knew he was beaten.

'What have you got there?' Clyde asked him, stunned.

'Joe reckons you can eat these,' Brian said. He smiled at Jane who gazed up at him adoringly.

'Christ, I meant the aborigines, not *us*. They know how to kill the damned things.'

'Oh, it's dead all right,' he said, and he threw it on the ground in front of us. 'Whacked it over the head with a stick. How about we gut it and stick it on the hot coals? Anyone got a knife?'

Next morning Joe was silent and morose all the way back to Preston. 'The man's a bloody maniac,' he whispered to me once. 'I can't compete.' He stole a wistful glance at the back of the Land-rover, where Brian and Jane sat curled in each other's arms. 'Just my luck. Just my rotten bloody luck.'

Brian came to the base before he left to go back to Perth. He wanted to thank us for inviting him along on the trip.

'Well, it was Joe's idea,' I told him.

'Think nothing of it,' Joe said.

'I appreciate it,' Brian said. 'You people have all been so friendly.' He turned to Joe. 'And thanks for all the tips on bushcraft. I guess it was lucky we had you along.'

'You're not so bad yourself,' Joe conceded.

'Well, I learned a thing or two from the old man. He was a Parks Ranger. I suppose growing up in the Kakadu helped a bit. Anyway, thanks again. See you around.'

25

Ken Ryan and the Great Ballantyne had never liked each other. They were too much alike in too many ways. Although Ryan would have never admitted it, they were both conspicuous individualists and they both enjoyed causing trouble. Ballantyne's practical jokes and Ryan's newspaper were expressions of the same need. Ballantyne and Ryan wanted to be loved, but neither had any real friends. Instead they had found a way to attract attention while further isolating themselves from their community.

They both enjoyed a captive audience. Everyone read the *Preston Bugle*, if only to ensure that their own name wasn't mentioned in it. They could then enjoy the litany of scurrilous lies and unsubstantiated rumour, complacent in the knowledge that they would not be the butt of local humour that week. But every Friday Ken Ryan would drink alone.

The Great Ballantyne, however, was never without companions. When he took up his post at the bar of the Union Hotel he was soon surrounded by admirers, eager to buy him a drink and offer him a smoke. In return he offered them free entertainment, and it was, after all, better to be in on the joke than be the butt of it. But his relationships were like a movie star's towards his loyal fans; he was at once idolized and remote.

Ryan had never forgiven Ballantyne for orchestrating the incident that had he and his beloved Ruperta ejected from the hotel. That following week he introduced another innovation to the local newspaper – a gossip column. It was less a column than a diatribe of vitriolic abuse, and it was directed mainly at Ballantyne and at Sergeant Dawson, who had fined Ryan the previous week for failure to give proper hand signals. Since the incident had occurred at night, Ryan's enmity was awakened. So much so, that he also initiated a 'Talking Health' column, which included a weekly update on the condition of Dawson's haemorrhoids. It was similar in style to a stock market report.

But it was at Ballantyne that the pith of Ryan's enmity was directed. He used the *Bugle* to speculate on the prankster's past life. The gossip column began to include teasers such as:

Which English resident is believed to have sought refuge in Australia after being charged with embezzling his grandmother?

A certain English resident, well known for his eccentricities, is reported to be involved in a law suit now taking place in London involving a brothel madam and a large sum of stolen money.

As Percy Ballantyne was the only English resident in the town at the time, it was quite clear at whom the libel was directed. But Ballantyne chose not to react. Instead, he took his revenge in his own inimitable style.

It was a Friday evening. Ryan assumed his usual post on a stool at the end of the bar, and settled down to read his own newspaper. Ballantyne, already in residence at the other end of the bar, surrounded by his sycophants, drained his glass and slammed it down on the bar.

'Nasty smell in here,' he said, leering in Ryan's direction. Ryan ignored him and Ballantyne walked out.

It seemed that everyone in town knew what was going to happen next except Ken Ryan. Ryan drove an ancient brown Chrysler Valiant, its chassis and bodywork eaten away by rust. It was parked outside, in the street. A few minutes later Ballantyne's thonged feet were seen protruding from underneath.

The plan was stunning in its simplicity. Ballantyne, who had been planning the ruse all week, had come prepared with a length of thin copper wire. He attached one end to a spark plug and ran the wire under the engine, and into the cabin through a rust hole in the floor. He then sticky-taped the other end of the wire to one of the seat springs, ensuring that a piece of the wire protruded through the vinyl seat.

The entire operation took less than ten minutes. When it was completed he re-entered the bar, to resume his prodigious consumption of free lager.

As the clock on the wall marched towards six o'clock, the atmosphere became charged with tension. Everyone fidgeted with anticipation. Ryan, however, seemed blissfully unaware of it.

Finally Ballantyne put down his drink, wiped his mouth with the back of his sleeve, and walked to the end of the bar where Ryan was seated. Ruperta sprang to her feet and growled, baring her yellow fangs.

Ryan looked up from his paper and scowled. 'What do you want?'

'Kenneth, old chap, I've come to kiss and make up.'

'You've what?'

'Life is but a short and fleeting thing. We should put away our barbs, old chap, and bring a little love into the world.'

'Piss off.'

'To show that I harbour no ill feelings about the way you've tried to besmirch my good name, I'd like to buy you a drink.'

Ryan looked as if he'd been slapped. 'You want to buy me a drink?'

'A peace offering, if you like.'

A sly grin smeared Ryan's putty brown face. 'Well, I reckon it's the least you owe me.'

'Quite right, old chap. What's your poison?'

Ryan considered a moment. He licked his lips. 'I'll have a triple Scotch.'

Ballantyne leaned on the bar and clicked his fingers.

'Gordon, old chap, let's have an extremely large Scotch for my good friend here.'

Gordon brought the Scotch and put it on the bar. He looked wary, 'Ye're no having this one on credit, Mister Ballantyne.'

Ballantyne reached into his pocket and pulled out a five dollar note. 'Wouldn't dream of it, old boy.'

Gordon took the money and held it up to the light. Satisfied it was genuine, he pushed the Scotch across the bar. Ryan grabbed the glass and swallowed the whisky in one gulp. His eyes watered as the strong spirit burned its way down his throat. He coughed, and Ballantyne patted him gently on the back.

'I guess you're not such a bad bastard after all,' Ryan conceded.

'Perish the thought.'

Ryan held out his hand. 'All right. We'll let bygones be bygones.'

Ballantyne shook his hand. 'Absolutely, old boy.'

Ryan looked up at the wall clock. It was almost six o'clock. 'Better be getting home for tea.' He got to his feet. The whisky had had an immediate effect and he was forced to lean on the bar for support.

'You all right, old chap?'

'I'm fine. Come on, Ruperta.' He staggered outside.

As soon as he was gone there was a rush for the windows. Those who couldn't get a position near a window stood on tables or chairs and craned their heads for a view. A breathless hush descended on the bar as Ryan opened his car door.

Ruperta got in first, and Ryan settled her in the passenger seat, on a cushion. Then he climbed in after her, slamming the door. He put the keys in the ignition. He paused a moment to run one hand over his face. He was not accustomed to sculling triple whiskies.

Bleary-eyed, he reached down and switched on the ignition.

Ryan's yell was heard in the public bar on the other side of the hotel. As the wire concealed beneath him shot its charge through his right buttock, he sprang out of his seat, his impetus baulked by the roof of the Valiant. Yelping with pain, he leaped out of the car, clutching his backside, and began hopping up and down in fright. He seemed to have no comprehension at all of what had happened to him.

Suddenly he became aware of the gales of mirth sweeping over him from the direction of the hotel bar. In fact, the saloon was in bedlam. Several of the audience had fallen from their perches on the tables and were rolling around the floor, holding their ribs. A few others were beating on the windows, pleading for Ryan to repeat the performance. Incredibly, he did.

His senses had been fogged by the alcohol. Aware only of the need for retreat, he jumped into his car, threw the gears into reverse and switched on the ignition. The car jumped backwards, and then stalled, as another charge lifted Ryan from his seat and sent him shrieking out of the driver's door once more.

The saloon bar was now a quivering mass of humanity. Howls of laughter echoed and rolled around the hotel. The only person seemingly unaffected was Ballantyne himself. He had not budged from the bar. He was casually working his way along the line of half-finished drinks, emptying the glasses.

Finally, reeling from this prodigious and rapid input of alcohol, he belched and staggered outside. There, he came face to face with Ken Ryan. He was standing on the sidewalk holding his backside with both hands, and quivering with rage and humiliation.

'What's this? A cabaret?' Ballantyne said.

Ryan was too stupefied with drink too work out what had happened to him. He only knew that Ballantyne was somehow responsible.

'Peace offering . . .' he spluttered. 'You bastard! The whole thing was just a bloody charade, wasn't it?'

'Of course it was,' Ballantyne told him.

'You don't want to be friends with me at all!'

'My dear chap. I'd rather make friends with a rattlesnake.'

'You made a fool of me!'

'That's no achievement.'

Ryan's hands clenched into fists at his side as he watched Ballantyne stagger away. 'I'll get even with you,' he hissed, 'I'll get even with you if it's the last thing I do!'

The vendetta might have continued unabated right through the Wet, thus providing months of amusement for the town, if it hadn't been for Nellie. Some said that Ryan paid her a straight bribe. Others reckoned he plied her with drinks one night in the Union Hotel. Perhaps she just decided to take revenge on him for the night he persuaded her to climb into my bed. Whatever the reason, Nellie conspired with the newspaper proprietor to obtain some of Ballantyne's private correspondence. She succeeded, and Ryan duly printed it.

There were three letters. One was from Ballantyne's father, flatly rejecting a plea for more cash. Another, purportedly from Ballantyne's sister, contained mostly abuse. The last, was a half-finished letter in Ballantyne's own handwriting. It was by far the most damaging. It was a letter to a friend of his, in London, and in it he expressed his contempt for the savagery of his surroundings and the collective ignorance and stupidity of his new companions.

Ken Ryan had struck a killer blow. The Great Ballantyne suddenly became a lonely figure at the Union Hotel.

It was half-past six. I was in the kitchen, making tea

and toast, when I heard someone rapping on the fly-screen door. I looked up. It was Ballantyne.

"Morning, old chap. Mind if I come in?"

'Of course. Pull up a chair.'

Ballantyne seemed to have lost his habitual swagger. He wore the pretence of a smile but his eyes were grey and sad. He had long ago discarded the outrageous blazer and tie, and now wore his usual uniform, a dirty white singlet and a pair of navy blue stubbies. He hadn't shaved.

He held up a bottle of beer. 'Brought some supplies with me.'

'Bit early in the morning for me. What about a cup of tea?'

Ballantyne slumped into a chair. 'I've heard tea's bad for your liver but oh well, why not?'

I put a mug of tea in front of him and sat down. 'You're up early.'

'Couldn't sleep, old chap.'

'Bad conscience?'

He didn't answer. He sipped his tea and ran his hand across the stubble on his chin. 'I'm going to fix that bloody Ryan.'

'Don't you think it's gone far enough?'

'Of course it has, old boy. Much too far. It's got to stop. But I'm going to fix him first.'

'You shouldn't have written those things,' I said as gently as I could. 'People round here are pretty sensitive to that sort of thing.'

'It was private!' Ballantyne hissed. 'He had no right to print it! I'm going to get even.'

'You did goad him into it.'

'What I did was harmless fun. Ryan was being . . . bloody malicious.' He took another sip of tea, and grimaced. 'This is revolting. Sure you don't want a beer?'

'No, thanks.'

200

'What time is it?'

'Twenty-five to seven.'

He stood up. 'Better be off, then. Don't want to miss Ryan's shower.'

'His what?'

Ballantyne grinned and leaned across the table, unnecessarily lowering his voice. Ryan lived a quarter of a mile away. 'Every morning about now he has a shower. I hide round the corner of his house till I hear the water running. I give him thirty seconds to get in and get soaped up, then I turn the water off at the mains. Bugger all he can do about it. Unless he gives up washing.' Rubbing his hands with anticipation he raced out, slamming the screen door behind him.

An hour later, I wandered outside into the warm morning sunshine, ready to drive to the base for the morning clinic. I heard someone groaning behind the frangipani tree. I went over to investigate. It was Ballantyne.

His right arm was wrapped in an old check shirt. It was soaked with blood. His face was a welter of deep, bloody scratches and there were more gashes on his bare chest and legs. Blood dripped down from the end of his fingers into the pool that was forming on the hardened red earth around his feet.

'Hello, old chap,' he said, his voice no more than a whisper. 'Just coming to see you. Be a good chap and and see if you can stop the bleeding, will you?'

When Sergeant Dawson saw me enter the police station, he suddenly became a very busy man. He took a file from the shelf behind him, turned his back and began to flick through the pages.

'Sergeant Dawson!'

'Yes . . . see to the gentleman, will you, Regan?'

Regan got up from his desk and came over. 'Hello,

Colin,' I said. 'Tell Sergeant Dawson I want to speak to him, will you?'

Regan shrugged his shoulders. 'Wants to speak to you, Sarge.'

Dawson looked irritated. 'Doctor Hubbard, isn't it?'

'Hazzard.'

'I'm very busy at the moment.'

'It's about Percy Ballantyne. I've just come from the hospital. He's had forty-eight stitches in an arm wound. One of the tendons has been severed and there's extensive nerve damage as well. He may even lose the use of his arm. We're flying him down to Perth tomorrow for more surgery.'

'Yes, yes, I'm very sorry to hear it. Give him my best regards, will you?'

'Your regards aren't worth two cents. What I want is some action.'

Dawson stuck his nose back into the file. 'It's not a police matter, Doctor.'

'That bloody dog should be destroyed. It's a menace.'

Dawson sucked his teeth with his tongue and considered. 'As I understand it, Mister Ballantyne was trespassing on Mister Ryan's property at the time.'

'So he was. That didn't give Ryan the right to set the dog on him.'

'It's not actually been proved that Ryan gave the dog the order to attack.'

'Ballantyne says he did.'

'Just one man's word against another's.'

'So you're just going to sit back and do nothing?'

Dawson straightened his shoulders and thrust out all three of his chins. 'There's no need to take that attitude.'

'The dog's a public menace. Ballantyne is the third person its attacked.'

'There's nothing I can do.'

'Well we both agree on that point, at least.' I went out, slamming the door behind me.

The next morning we ferried Percy Ballantyne to Broome. An aerial ambulance was to be flown up from Carnarvon and from there he was to be taken to the Royal Perth Hospital. The surgeon at Preston had confided to me that he feared Ballantyne might lose all use of the arm.

Ballantyne lay on the stretcher in the rear of the cabin as we soared over the vast pindan plain between Preston and Broome. It was still the Dry season, and ahead of us there were the black charcoal strokes of bush fires raging on the plain, ink smudges on the pale blue sky.

I took some clinic calls over the radio, then went to the rear and checked on my patient. 'How are you feeling?'

'Not too bad, old chap. Have to learn to drink with my left hand, won't I?'

'They'll fix you up in Perth.'

'Jolly good.' He smiled. He'd lost a lot of blood and was still very pale. But they'd bathed and shaved him at the hospital, and with the lank hair pushed back from his face, I momentarily glimpsed someone else, a pale, blond young man with a calm, sensitive face and intelligent eyes.

'What happened to you, Percy?'

'Got bitten by a dog, old boy.'

'You know what I mean. What brought you all the way out here?'

He looked up at the ceiling. 'Tale of lost love and debauchery, old chap. Very boring, really.'

'Come on. Drop the act. Its looking a bit thin with a drip in your arm.'

He looked at me, surprised. 'It's not very interesting. Just another lost soul on the run.'

'From what?'

'Heard of Eton?'

'That's the English equivalent of Melbourne Grammar, isn't it?'

Ballantyne raised his eyebrows. 'Good heavens, no. You don't have anything even remotely similar in this brown and unpleasant land. Eton is the English equivalent of the school God went to.'

'You're a graduate.'

'A dux. After Eton, I was at Oxford. Read the classics. I was set to enter the Diplomatic Corps. My father was Ambassador to the United States of America.'

'You dropped out?'

Ballantyne shook his head. He fell silent for a while. 'I made the terrible mistake of falling in love with a girl who worked in a coffee shop in Oxford High Street. We were going to get married. She got pregnant, you see.'

I guessed what was coming. 'Your father stopped you.'

'No, he didn't stop me. He stopped her. Ten thousand pounds, I think was the sum. I don't know who I hated more. Him for offering it, or her for taking it.'

'Perhaps,' I said after a while, 'perhaps she was just after the money all along.'

If Ballantyne had not been lying on the stretcher, I think he would have struck me. His eyes blazed. 'I refuse to believe that.' He turned his head away. 'After she left, I resolved to make my father's life as miserable as possible. I believe I have succeeded admirably up till now, in that he is utterly and thoroughly ashamed of me. It's his reward for teaching me the price of love. Ten thousand pounds. It was actually considerably less in Nellie's case, I believe, but then that was only friendship.'

'You can't carry this bitterness through life for ever,' I murmured.

I thought I might have my first real dialogue with this strange and troubled young man, but when he turned back to me the look of cocksure mischief had returned. 'Oh, I don't know,' he said cheerfully. 'I reckon I can make a damned good fist of it.'

Ballantyne never came back to Preston, not even to collect the meagre belongings he had left behind in the rented house. After extensive surgery in Perth he regained partial use of his arm, and the last I heard of him was from a nurse at the Preston hospital who had worked on his ward in Perth. She remembered him clearly, for he was suspected of being responsible for defacing the name cards over fellow patients' beds. One morning the nurses had been summoned by alarmed patients who had found 'SMITH – GONER', or 'WELLS – NO HOPE', and even 'SIMPSON – CASTRATE AND PRAY FOR THE BEST' hanging over their beds. When Ballantyne was transferred to Shenton Park to convalesce the mysterious outbreak of practical joking ceased.

No one in the Kimberley ever saw the Great Ballantyne again. It's a big world, after all, and there are plenty of places to hide.

26

I heard the tyres of the Land-rover crunch on the gravel and I looked outside. The familiar beanbag figure of Sergeant Dawson slopped out of the front seat onto the ground. Hitching up the khaki trousers that seemed almost to break and strain like sail canvas beneath their weighty load, he sauntered towards the radio hut.

'It's that rotten copper,' Clyde said, and turned back to the radio.

I had just finished my morning clinic. I put down the last of my file cards, got up and went outside. 'Hello, Sergeant.'

'Doctor Hubbard, I was hoping I'd find you here.'

'It's Hazzard.'

'Yes, of course.' He put his hands on his hips and sniffed. He looked up at the sky. 'Nice morning.'

Since the weather during the Dry season is monotonously similar, this was not a scintillating gambit. 'Yes, it is.'

He stuck a thumb up his left nostril. 'How's that bloke who used to live next door to you. What was his name? Ballantyne.'

'I don't know. He was discharged from the Royal Perth Hospital a few weeks ago. Haven't heard anything since.'

'His arm all right?'

'Not really.'

'Shame.'

I was growing impatient. 'What can I do for you, Sergeant?'

'Got some news for you.'

I waited. 'Go on.'

'That dog that did it. It died yesterday.'

'Ryan's dog? The bull terrier?'

'That's the one.' He clicked his fingers. 'Went just like that.'

'I'm relieved to hear it. I still say it should have been put down. It was a monster.'

'That's what everyone says.'

'What happened to it?'

Dawson shrugged his massive shoulders. 'It was just sort of running along the road, and suddenly it just kind of stopped, its eyes bulged out of his head and it gave this funny sort of yelp. And it died. That was it.'

'Good heavens. That was sudden. I wonder what caused it.'

'Dunno,' Dawson said. 'Maybe it was my Land-rover going over the top of it. Anyway, mustn't hold you up. I know you're a busy man.' And he got back inside his vehicle and drove off. I stared after him. He had just revived my faith in human nature.

Just after Christmas Jane Goodluck left Preston to return to Perth and marry Brian. 'It's about time I went back,' she told us in a rare moment of candour as we flew back from a clinic. 'I'll have to rescue him from all those other girls.'

Joe's head whipped around. 'You mean . . . he's . . . well . . . he's got other girlfriends?'

'I'm afraid so. I don't think he can help it. It's just the way he's made, I suppose.'

Joe stared at her aghast. The idea that a man would have Jane Goodluck and still want other women had not occurred to him. 'What a bastard.'

'Don't you dare say that!' Jane's violet eyes blazed. 'He is not a bastard! You apologize this instant!'

'Sorry,' Joe mumbled.

We were all at the airport the day she left. Clyde

and I shook her hand and wished her well. Joe patiently waited his turn.

'Good luck, Goodluck,' I said.

'Thanks, Mike. I've enjoyed it. You've all been wonderful.'

'Yairs, well, you make sure you come back and see us.' Clyde told her.

'I will.' She kissed us both on the cheek and quickly turned and headed for the exit gate.

'Wait a minute,' Joe said, desperately.

'Joe! Sorry. I nearly forgot you. It's all the excitement of knowing I'll be seeing Brian again soon.'

I saw Joe gulp at this final insult. Jane didn't notice. She held out her hand. 'Goodbye.'

Joe took a deep breath. 'I love you,' he whispered.

An Avro Anson from Carnarvon had just landed on the runway. The roar of its engine drowned out every other sound. 'What?'

'I love you.'

'I can't hear!'

'I SAID I LOVE YOU!'

Jane laughed and shook her head. 'You're silly,' she told him, and turned and walked off towards her aircraft and out of Joe's life. Joe watched her go, and then without a word he shrugged past me and walked towards the car park.

It was the final blow. He had finally summoned the courage to tell her how he felt and Jane Goodluck hadn't even taken him seriously enough to reject him.

27

Like many other large property owners, Gerry Foulkes had a mobile transceiver mounted in his F–100. It proved to be an invaluable asset when he blew up the homestead and destroyed the principal set.

I was at the residence when the phone rang. It was Clyde. 'Yairs, g'day, Doc. Got Gerry on the radio. Seems he's had a bit of a nasty accident.'

'What's happened?'

'I'll put him on. You can have a chat to him yourself.'

Clyde patched Gerry through on the land-line. I heard the crackle of static over the phone. 'Gerry? It's Doctor Hazzard. What appears to be the problem? Over.'

'Come a proper gutzer this time,' Gerry shouted down the line. 'The house has gone.'

'Can you repeat, Gerry? Over.'

'The bloody house has gone. It's Molly's fault. She shouldn't have lit the bloody oven. Ker-ist, what a mess.'

'What's happened, Gerry? Is anyone hurt?'

'The War Office got a bit hysterical. Had to lay 'er out. Shit, she panics, that woman. Maybe you ought to come and get 'er. I reckon she's gone psychomolog-ical, just like you said.'

There was never any doubt in my mind that an evacuation was required. But what did Gerry mean, 'the house has gone'?

'Where are you now, Gerry? Over.'

'I'm in the Land-rover, right by the 'ouse. What's left of the damned place. Bloody woman. Fancy lightin' the oven when I told 'er not to.'

'Stand by, Gerry. I'll give you an ETA as soon as we're airborne. And for God's sake, don't hit Molly again. You don't know your own strength. Over.'

Eugene was waiting for us at the airstrip in the red Commer. Sam and I hurried over and jumped into the front seat beside him. 'How's your mother?' I asked him.

'Out to it,' Eugene said, crunching the truck into first without using the clutch. 'The old man gave her a fair whack.'

'I hope he hasn't done her any serious harm.'

'He had to do something. She was trying to skitch 'im with the wood axe.'

We bounced back along the rutted red track towards Invercargill or, that is, to where Invercargill had once been. All that was left was the blackened shell of the walls. The tin roof had been blasted away and the gnarled and twisted metal was spread over an area of half a mile. The ground was littered with debris, pieces of furniture, glass, and charred cloth. I got out of the cab and looked around. The blackened pages of a tattered recipe book blew in the dusty breeze.

Sam gave Gerry a huge grin. 'How you goin', you old bastard?'

Gerry was not in a good temper. 'How do you think I'm goin'? Me 'ome's cactus and me missus has gone troppo. How do you think I'm bloody goin'?'

'For God's sake, what happened?' I asked him.

'Like I said, it was 'er fault. I was warming up some gelly in the oven. Stupid bloody woman must 'ave lit it and closed the door. I bloody told 'er!'

'You had gelignite in the oven again?'

'It's a lot easier to use when it's a bit warm.'

'Is anyone injured?'

'Nar, it was lucky. Eugene was with me, and the War Office was over in the store when it blew. No sign of Lucky though. Reckon he must have still been in the house. He used to like to sleep next to the hand-grenades.'

'The hand-grenades? You kept them in the house?'

'They was under the bed.' He noticed my look of stunned amazement. 'Well, I didn't want no bastard nicking them.'

'Where's Molly?'

Gerry led me towards the banana palm at the edge of the garden. The force of the blast had snapped off many of the branches, and they lay littered around the base of the tree. Molly Foulkes lay against the trunk, conscious now, gingerly rubbing the livid bruise on her cheek with her fingertips. Her eyes stared vacantly into the middle distance. She was trembling violently.

I bent down. 'Molly? Are you all right? It's me, Doctor Hazzard.' She looked around and almost managed a child-like smile. The swelling on her cheek had almost closed one eye.

'Sorry I 'ad to hit you, pet,' Gerry said. 'You feelin' okay now?'

At the sound of his voice Molly stiffened and her face curled into a snarl. 'Get that idiot away from me. Get him away!' Then her face seemed to dissolve, melting into a grimace. 'Please go away!' She made a feeble attempt to strike him with her open hand and doubled over, sobbing.

'Jeez, what have I done?' Gerry said.

I reached out, and cradled Molly in my arms. 'She's in shock,' I said. 'Help me get her to the truck, Sam.'

Gerry took a pace forward.

'No, not you, Gerry. I'm sorry, but it will only make things worse.'

Gerry shook his head. 'I dunno. That's the trouble with bloody women. They get so bloody emotional.'

As Molly recounted the story to me later, Gerry had

never mentioned leaving the gelignite in the oven range. She put a roast in, slammed the door and then went over to the store to check on provisions. The Wet was on the way and they would have to stock up for the long months ahead.

The next thing she remembered was the bang and being knocked to the floor as the walls of the store buckled under the force of the blast. She had thought for a moment that the aluminium shed was about to collapse on top of her. It warped and twisted, but thankfully remained upright. There was another massive concussion as the grenades exploded too.

When she finally staggered outside she found her home littered across a half-mile radius. Black smoke billowed into the air from the burning kitchen. Too stunned to move or speak, she could only stand and watch as the fire gutted what remained of the homestead.

A few minutes later Gerry returned in the Land-rover. She remembered him leaping down from the running board and running towards her, arms outstretched. 'Its all right, pet,' he shouted. 'Don't worry. I'm okay.'

That's when she ran to fetch the wood axe.

A sliver of moon hung over the pink walls of the gorge. I turned off the engine of the Land-rover and climbed out of the cabin. From somewhere among the eucalypts, a crow uttered his plaintive call. It echoed around the walls, hanging on the still evening air. George came and stood behind me. We both stared in sullen grief at the wire fence.

PRIVATE PROPERTY
NO TRESSPASSING
Aminex Corp.

'They can't do this,' I heard myself saying.

George just shrugged his shoulders. 'Mebbe we try Simpson Gorge,' he said. 'We catch bream, mebbe trevally.'

'George, they can't mine around here. It's . . . they can't.' George was silent. I turned and walked back to the Land-rover. 'You drive,' I said. I slumped into the passenger seat. I felt as if someone had just punched me in the stomach.

'A place like this. They shouldn't be able to fence it off.'

'Yo-i, boss.'

'Doesn't it bother you?'

It was a stupid remark. I suppose I just wanted to goad him into a reaction. His brown eyes stared at me in reproach. 'Guess I just doan get angry 'bout it no more.'

'They've fenced us out.'

'Yo-i.'

'Has this happened to you before?'

'Sure, boss.' George started the engine.

'Where?'

George shrugged his shoulders. 'The Kimberley,' he said.

We drove away.

28

I had come to accept that Mrs Denison didn't like me. After the incident over the fruit cake her paranoia grew worse than before. She circulated rumours that I was trying to poison her.

Her two most loved possessions were her cats, Blackie and Chalkie. Blackie often went walkabout for days on end, and the old lady would always contrive to link his disapperance with my supposed malevolence. She told anyone who would listen that I had either kidnapped him or had murdered him to satisfy some secret bloodlust.

It would have taken a far braver man than me to capture the redoubtable Blackie. He was a fearsome looking beast, with a scarred and battered face, yellow fangs and a sour temper. Mrs Denison was the only human being he allowed within ten feet of him.

One morning, on the way to the base, I found him lying in the middle of the road, outside the old woman's house. He was horribly mutilated. He had evidently been too slow to avoid a passing car. Like a fool, I stopped and wrapped Blackie's corpse in an old towel from the boot of my Holden. I then knocked on Mrs Denison's door. It was my intention to try and break the bad news to her as gently as possible, rather than have her simply find her beloved cat's body herself later that morning.

Mrs Denison wasn't an appealing sight at that hour of the day. She had had no time to put in her dentures and her sparse grey hair stuck out from her head like the bristles on an emu. She threw open the door and gave a small shriek when she recognized me. She took

214

a step back and pulled the thin woollen dressing gown tight around her throat.

'What do you want?'

'Mrs Denison. It's about Blackie.'

Her demented gaze dropped to the pathetic bundle I carried in my arms. One black paw protruded from the bloodied towel. Her jaw dropped, the bottom lip quivered in rage and fear. 'You've killed my cat.'

'No, Mrs Denison, I found him in the road—'

'YOU KILLED MY CAT!'

'No, please listen, what happened was, I was driving—'

'CAT MURDERER!'

Too late, I realized the tragic error I had made in not leaving Blackie in the road to collect a few more tyre marks. Cursing myself for a fool, I laid Blackie's body on the front step and ran for the gate. The damage had been done. There was nothing left to do but retreat.

Ryan had a field day with Mrs Denison's fevered reconstruction of the incident, when she relayed it to him later that morning. It appeared in the next edition of the *Preston Bugle* as 'FLYING DOCTOR MURDERS PENSIONER'S PET FOR MEDICAL RESEARCH'. Once again, I threatened to sue. Fortunately, no one in town took it seriously. It was merely reckoned a wonderful running joke, albeit at my expense.

Naturally enough, when the chance came to redeem myself, I leaped at the opportunity. Among the few possessions that the Great Ballantyne left behind was Roger, the carpet snake. When Percy failed to return to the house, Roger grew hungry and contrived to escape from the wooden box that had been his home. However, he must have anticipated Percy's return, because he didn't wander far from his home, and one afternoon Mrs Denison found him curled up in the sun on her back step.

They probably heard her scream in Darwin. George came rushing in from the back garden with a look of terror on his face. 'Sound like a bunyip, boss,' he said. He was only half joking. Behind him Ethel nibbled in agitation at the fly wire, her comic head cocked in surprise towards the source of the screams.

Thinking she had slipped and broken a bone I dashed out of the back door and vaulted the two fences that separated her house from my own. Expecting to find her prostrate on the ground, I was surprised to see her instead crouching in terror behind the fly wire door, clutching her broom for protection and pointing with one trembling hand at Roger, who lay coiled and basking in the sun, seemingly oblivious to the panic he had caused.

'It's a Rattle Constrictor,' the old lady shouted, in a tremulous voice. 'Help me!'

At once I saw my opportunity to raise my stocks with my irksome neighbour. 'It's all right,' I said. 'I'll save you.'

'Let him eat you,' she suggested. 'Then maybe he'll go away and leave me alone.'

Roger, disturbed from his siesta by the sudden movement around him, began to slither away off the step to find a dark and quiet corner under the house. Quickly, I reached out, grabbed him by the tail and carried him, still wriggling, around the side of the house. I deposited him in an empty wooden box outside Ballantyne's house, making a mental note to collect him later and set him free somewhere in the bush.

'It's all right,' I shouted to the old woman. 'You're safe now. I've saved your life.'

Mrs Denison was effusive in her thanks. She wasn't to know that Roger was quite harmless. I certainly wasn't going to tell her.

The next day she went to the offices of the *Preston Bugle* and relayed the story of my heroic deed to Ken

Ryan, but of course it never found its way into the paper. Ken, like newspapermen everywhere, was not interested in good news. It doesn't sell newspapers.

I wasn't worried. Mrs Denison and I had become the best of neighbours. She presented me with a home-made steak pie and brought the beloved Chalkie around to see me. She even allowed me to stroke him. It was a great honour.

Then one morning, as I was on my way to the aero-drome, something white and small raced out from Mrs Denison's house and I felt a terrible crunch as it disappeared under the wheels of the Holden. Shaking with apprehension I stopped the car and got out. Chalkie lay in the middle of the road, quite dead.

I hesitated. What should I do? I knew what I *wasn't* going to do; present the corpse to the old lady. Instead I lifted up the body, placed it gently on the kerbside and got back in the car. I drove off.

Then I heard a shout and I glanced in my rear vision mirror. I caught a glimpse of an old toothless woman in a woollen dressing gown standing over the body of the dead cat and waving her fist at me. It was Mrs Denison.

'Oh well,' I told myself, 'it was nice while it lasted,' and spent the rest of the week dreading the next issue of the *Preston Bugle*.

It was late afternoon when I got back to the Residence after the flight to Barker Downs. A stockman had been injured in a muster when his horse had lost its footing and fallen, crushing him under it. He had broken his leg in two places, cracked several ribs and had a bad concussion. On the way back we had received another emergency medical call, this time at Benowra, for an aboriginal woman with a post-partum haemorrhage. By the time I got back to Preston I was exhausted. I threw open the door and headed for the kitchen.

'Hello, Mike.'

'David,' I stopped and gaped in surprise.

The fair-haired man in the grey woollen trousers and white cotton shirt stood up and held out his hand. 'Been a long time.'

'What are you doing here? . . I . . . you should have let me know you were coming.'

'Didn't know myself. I was in Perth for a convention and it finished early. Thought I'd shoot up here and say hello.'

I stared at him. It was like looking at a ghost. Perhaps, in some ways, I was, for David was a spectre from another life, a life I had left behind to come to the bush. We had studied together at medical school, and had remained firm friends when we went our own ways in private practice. He and his wife had helped to keep me sane after the loss of my wife and son.

'You're looking brown,' he grinned. 'Been out wrestling crocodiles?'

'Couldn't find any. Had to settle for tiger snakes.'

'I'm impressed.'

'Want a beer?'

'You're friend George had already been helping me get the dust out of my throat.' I hadn't noticed George sitting behind me at the kitchen table. He grinned, and picked up a half-empty bottle in the middle of the table and refilled two glasses.

'I'll get another glass, boss,' he said.

'Thanks, George.' I turned back to David. 'I can't believe it's you. It's good to see you again. How long are you here for?'

'Have to catch the flight back tomorrow morning. As I said, it really is just a flying visit.'

'Well don't expect much sleep tonight then,' I told him. 'We've got a lot of catching up to do.'

Later that evening we strolled down towards the jetty.

The sun was low in the sky and the worst of the heat was over. David mopped at his neck and face with a handkerchief. 'Is it always like this?' he asked me.

'This cool, you mean?'

'You call this "cool"?'

'You get used to it. Well, no, you don't really get used to it. But I suppose you forget what it's like down south.'

We had reached the jetty. On either side the marshes shimmered in the late sun, a flat expanse of dirty brown and dark green. 'I didn't just come up to say hello, you know,' David said, suddenly.

'I had a feeling there was something else.'

'Is it that obvious?'

'I've known you for a long time.'

'Old Fred Hobday's retiring next month. That'll leave just me and Geoff Walters. The practice is too busy for just the two of us.'

'I see.'

'I know you can't just pack up and leave. But . . . well, I guess you must have given some thought to the future.' He seemed to be waiting for me to say something. When I didn't he went on. 'Obviously you don't have to give me an answer now. But . . . well, I suppose I'd like to have some idea of what you're planning. It would be great to see you back in Sydney again.'

I stopped walking and sat down on the edge of the jetty. 'I don't know.'

'You can't stay up here for ever. Good God, Mike, you know what happens to doctors who stay in the bush too long. They get stuck into the drink.'

'It's not so bad,' I murmured.

'You're not going to tell me you enjoy it up here? Mike, this is the end of the world. You might as well be living in Mongolia.'

I didn't answer him. It was impossible to explain,

this strange affinity to such an inhospitable place. Instead I said: 'You know what day it is tomorrow?'

David turned away, embarrassed. 'Yes, I remember. It wasn't deliberate.'

'Yes, I know.' Tomorrow it would be exactly four years since Angela and Steven had died. By now he would have been going to school.

'You have to try and leave it behind, Mike.'

'I thought I had,' I said. It was true. I thought I had forgotten. But now it seemed that all I had done was push it out of my consciousness, like jamming down the lid on a boiling pot. It was still there, simmering.

'I heard you'd got yourself engaged.'

'It fell through.'

We were silent for a while. 'So what are your plans?'

'I really don't know.'

'For God's sake, Mike, you've got a life to live. You have to go on with it.'

I didn't know what to say. Was he right? Was I hiding up here? Was it simply easier to forget that the other life had never happened so that I could forget my grief? Was it also perhaps the reason I had allowed Megan to slip away from me, and had then been content to blame it on circumstance? 'I'll think about it, David,' I said. 'I promise.'

'I worry about you, sometimes.'

I stood up. It was getting towards evening. The mosquitoes would be out in pursuit soon. 'Let's be getting back. You can have a shower and some tea and I'll show you the nightlife.'

'You've got nightlife?' David said.

'This place buzzes on a Friday night. By the way – have you ever seen *The African Queen?*'

29

The morning and afternoon clinic sessions over the radio were a vital part of my everyday routine. As my patients could not come to my surgery, as they would in the city, the consultations would take place over the radio. Each Flying Doctor has his own technique for diagnosing symptoms accurately over the air, but the onus is on the patients to use their senses in place of the physicians. The medical kits provided by the Royal Flying Doctor also had a stylized anatomical chart to help patients locate the exact part of the body where they were experiencing their discomfort. Numbers denoted specific areas on the front of the body, letters for the back.

This system of consultation has only one obvious drawback. Sometimes a patient may feel their condition is of just too sensitive a nature to broadcast thousands of square miles across the north-west, and they may travel long distances in order to attend a remote outpost clinic and retain their privacy.

One morning I was sitting in the radio hut at the base, going through the usual routine of the clinic. I was talking to the wife of the manager of Durban Downs, and her case was proving to be a difficult one.

'Can you describe the pain exactly, Mrs Thompson. Is it a sharp pain or a dull ache?'

'It sort of starts as a dull ache, then goes to a sharp pain, then just sorts of throbs a bit.'

'Where exactly do you experience this discomfort, Mrs Thompson? Can you use the chart in the medicine chest?'

'Well, the pain starts at number two, then sort of

shoots down to number eleven, slides sideways to twelve, shoots up to six, then finishes as a sort of dull throbbing achey pain in number four.'

It was almost a relief to receive the emergency call.

'Six Victor Sarah Brookton, medical call. Six Victor Sarah Brookton, medical call.'

I recognized Sean's voice immediately. Mrs Thompson ended her litany of achey painy throbs and a silence fell, broken only by the crackle of static. I switched the transceiver to 'transmit'. 'Flying Doctor answering Six Victor Sarah. Go ahead with your message, Sean.'

'We have an emergency here, Doctor. Request immediate assistance.'

'Can you describe the nature of the emergency for me, please. Over.' For long seconds there was only the crackle of the carrier wave. 'I repeat. Can you describe the nature of the emergency for me. Over.'

'It's . . . well . . . one of the men . . . one of the best men at the station, in fact . . . is in great distress.'

'What appears to be the problem? Over.'

Just the whine and crackle of the carrier wave. Then: 'Look, Doctor, can you just trust my judgement on this?'

I started to lose patience. 'Can you bring Miss Hoagan to the radio, please?'

'Mike, please. For God's sake. This isn't the sort of thing I can discuss over the radio. For old time's sake, eh?'

I thought about the old times Sean and I had shared and decided the remark showed poor salesmanship on Sean's part. 'I'm afraid you'll have to describe the symptoms to me in greater detail, 6VS. Or wait for tomorrow afternoon's clinic. Over.'

'Six Victor Sarah to Flying Doctor. Over and out. Shithead!'

I continued with my morning clinicals.

*

The next day Sam and I took off from Preston aerodrome to conduct a number of clinics in the West Kimberley. Later that afternoon, we arrived at Brookton. I looked forward to the clinic with a mixture of curiosity and amusement. The previous day's radio conversation with Sean had left me speculating on why he had felt unable to describe his ailment over the air. Venereal disease? Surely not. However, it would explain his reticence to discuss the symptoms. Yet that particular affliction would not have compelled him to request an emergency flight. Haemorrhoids? That would be equally delightful, but again, not particularly urgent. The anticipation of the afternoon's clinic left me with a feeling of delicious anticipation.

Sure enough, Sean had ensured that he was first in line that morning. He shut the door firmly behind him and glared at me in impotent rage. 'Ive been in agony for almost twenty-four hours, thanks to you.'

I took out a file card and waved him to a chair. 'How do you spell your surname. With or without a *p?*'

He limped into the room. I stared at him, puzzled. 'What are you wearing your poncho for? The Wet's almost a month away.'

'It's your bloody fault.' He sat down and rested his elbows on his knees, doubled over with pain. 'If the other blokes find out about this, I'm history. I'll never live it down.'

Slowly, painfully, he lifted the poncho over his head. He was wearing a long check shirt, outside his jeans, so that it covered his crotch. He lifted it gingerly and pointed. 'Bloody thing's caught in the zipper. I tried to get it out myself but it only made it worse.'

I had discovered the true meaning of bliss. It required a superhuman effort on my part to retain an expression of professional detachment as I bent to examine the swollen and captive organ. The foreskin had somehow become caught in the zipper of his jeans. It must have been excrutiatingly painful.

'Oh dear,' I muttered. 'Oh dear, oh dear.'

'Can you do something?'

'I don't know. When did this happen?'

'Yesterday afternoon.'

'You've left it a terribly long time,' I lied. 'It could be infected. I'll have to cut away the necrosis.'

Sean blanched. 'You're not cutting anything.'

I looked into his face. 'Only a small part. You'll still be able to use it to pee out of.'

'Cut it out, Mike.'

'If you prefer.'

'Stop kidding around. Just do something, will you?'

He was frantic. The pain and humiliation had become etched into the tanned and handsome face, and he looked strangely frail. It was a wonderful moment. 'It's going to be incredibly painful.' *I hope.*

'You can give me a local anaesthetic, can't you?'

'I don't mean now. Later.'

'Just get the damn thing out.'

'All right. Lie down on the kitchen table. We'll see what we can do.'

Sean got painfully to his feet and hobbled to the table. He eased himself fearfully onto the edge and lay back. I took a scalpel out of the medical kit and held it casually in my right hand. 'Wish I'd known about this. I wouldn't have had all those beers last night. Gives me a touch of the shakes.'

Sean had turned white. 'For God's sake. This isn't funny.'

I slipped on a pair of rubber gloves. 'Don't want to get blood all over my hands,' I told him cheerfully. I held the scalpel under his nose, letting the sunlight that flooded in through the open window reflect on the steel blade. I bent over. 'Now then. Where is it?'

'Ha, ha.'

'Hmmm . . . hardly seems worth worrying about.'

'Look, you've had your little joke. Get on with it.'

'Talking of jokes, my neighbour told me you paid him ten dollars to put a girl in my bed while I was out with Megan. Or perhaps you don't want to talk about it right now.'

'Mike I–'

'Now just lie back and try to relax . . .'

I was packing away the kit at the end of the clinic when Megan walked in. 'Hello.'

'Hi.'

'Everything okay?'

'Usual thing. A few septic fingers, some bruised ribs and a twisted ankle. Not a sign of any more bush remedies.'

'You won't have any more trouble there.'

'By the way, what was wrong with Sean? He's been acting very strange all morning.'

'He's all fixed now. Probably be a bit sore for a few days.'

'What was wrong with him?'

'I can't really tell you. Professional ethics.'

'Nothing to worry about, I hope?'

'Oh, no. Certainly nothing to worry about. In fact it was just a little thing, really.'

It was the morning after Father Tom Pallenberg lost his right hand trying to climb on the back of a saltwater crocodile.

We took off at first light. As we flew north-west a single night star still blazed in the sky in front of us, like a beacon. A watery blue seeped across the sky.

'Hope the strip's dried out,' I said.

'It probably hasn't,' Joe muttered.

I turned round in the cockpit to watch the dawn. The horizon deepened through yellow to orange and then to a rich blood red. Finally a piercing golden shaft of light knifed through the clouds as the sun rose.

'Another hot day,' Joe said.

'Yes,' I agreed. 'Another hot day.' I wondered how long you had to live in this country before you got used to the oppressive heat, if you ever came to watch a sunrise without dread for the coming day. Perhaps you never got used to it.

'Yep,' Joe murmured, 'another hot bloody horrible day in my rotten life.'

The Wet had broken but there had been no rain for two days and Joe had been assured by Parrot Island that the strip on Cape Leveque was clear for use. We had received the call from them just after midnight but Joe had discounted any possibility of a night flight. 'Not on that strip,' he told me, 'that would be pushing my luck too far.'

We crossed the fringe of mangroves and spotted the dry scar of the airfield dead ahead of us. Joe made a low pass to satisfy himself that the strip was serviceable. As we flew over, I saw the Land-rover parked on the edge of the dirt runway and three figures standing by the open passenger door.

As we made our final approach I felt the plane being buffeted by the crosswinds. 'Say your prayers,' Joe muttered. 'It's all over for us.'

I felt my fingers tighten around the edge of my seat as the ground rose to meet us. After my earlier apprehension it was something of an anti-climax. Joe made a perfect three-point landing and we taxied across to the parked Land-rover. I went to the rear cabin door and jumped down.

Tom Pallenberg was sitting on the running board of the Land-rover, his left hand soaked in a blood-stained bandage. His shirt and trousers were also covered in blood. Two of the Parrot Islanders were standing over him.

'What happened?'

Tom looked up and smiled an apology. He was deathly pale. 'Hello, young fella. Sorry to bring you out here like this, but I seem to have mislaid some fingers.'

I unwrapped the sodden bandages. Half the hand was gone. 'What the hell have you been doing?'

'He think he got im boat,' one of the men said. 'No more, no more. He got im crocydile.'

'It was dark, you see,' Tom said. 'I was going out to check on our nets. Silly place to leave a damned crocodile.'

'What happened? Did you tread on it?'

'No, I'm afraid I tried to launch it.'

'Come on, we'll get you onto the plane.'

'Cheer up, Mike. It could have been worse. Could have been my old fella.'

30

It was a watery blue sky. We soared high over the Stirling Sound, the sun glinting on the aluminium sheds of the aerodrome below us. Sam banked the plane to starboard over the marshes towards the brown haze of the Kimberley. The Cessna's shadow dwindled to a speck on the ground below us.

We flew for a while in silence, each lost in our own thoughts. Finally, Sam said: 'You're thinking of going back to Sydney.'

'Who told you that?'

'Clyde.'

'I don't know why I talk to that man. I might as well put a notice in the paper and save him the trouble of telling everyone.'

'I didn't know it was a secret.'

'It's just that I haven't made up my mind what I'm going to do.'

Sam turned to look at me. 'It's a girl, isn't it?'

'Some of it is. It's just . . . well, I'd always planned to go back. Now seems like a good time, I suppose. Except . . .'

'Except?'

'Except I don't want to leave.'

'Don't then.'

'I don't know. It doesn't seem that simple.'

Sam became suddenly serious. I suppose I had pigeon-holed him as a bit of a comic turn, and I had never suspected another side to him. 'You can't go back, Mike. Once you leave somewhere, that's it. You go back and it's like living in a picture album.'

'How do you mean?'

'I went back to Nagasaki once. I don't know why. I'd been living in San Francisco for ten years and all my family was dead. I suppose I still thought of myself as a prisoner of war. But Japan had changed, and I'd changed. I suppose I've still never quite accepted it, but it gets easier with time.'

'I don't exactly see myself as a prisoner of war.'

'No, but a prisoner of circumstance perhaps.'

He had a point. I wasn't sure. Could I go back? Should I? Or was it just running away all over again?

Molly Foulkes sat in my kitchen, nursing a cold cup of tea. 'It's no good, Doctor,' she was saying, 'I can't go back to him. Not now. Not ever.'

I fidgeted in my chair. I had not been trained either as a counsellor or a psychiatrist. Molly had just spent a week in the local hospital being treated for shock. The week alone on the shaded verandahs among the mangoes and poinsettias had obviously convinced her she should leave her husband. I could not be sure that her recent trauma had dislodged the balance of her mind, or perhaps restored it.

Gerry had made constant enquiries after his wife during the morning and afternoon clinics. In my innocence, I had informed him that Molly would be returning to Invercargill the next day. He had sounded excited. It was almost as if he had missed her.

'I want you to tell him for me,' Molly went on.

'I can't do that, Molly. This is something you ought to tell him yourself.'

'I can't. I'm scared of what he might do.'

'You can't just run off. You've been married a long time.'

'He's mad. I used to think he was funny, but he's not. He's not all there. He ought to be put away for his own good.'

I sighed. 'What exactly do you want me to say to him?'

'Just tell him. You're over there for the clinic next week. You can tell him then.'

'What about Eugene?'

She shrugged. 'I don't care. I don't care about either of 'em. He's just like his father. He doesn't need me.'

'He's only ten years old.'

'I'm gettin' the bus down to Perth this afternoon. Nothing's going to stop me, Doctor. I mean it.'

I believed her. She had a look of desperation about her. There were dark rings under her eyes, and she fidgeted endlessly with her fingers, pulling and tugging at the gold band on the third finger of her left hand. It was as if she was acting out the struggle taking place inside her.

'What if I refuse?'

'I'm not going back. This is the first time I've got away from him in years. If I go back now, he'll persuade me to stay. And then the only way I'll ever get away from him is in a pine box.'

'What about writing him a letter, at least?'

'Can't write.'

'You could dictate one to me.'

'There's nothing to say. Just tell him I've gone. That's it.' She pushed the cold tea away from her and stood up. 'I have to go. I don't want to miss the bus.'

I suddenly felt very sorry for her. It was easy to be critical of what she was doing, but then perhaps Gerry had deserved it. He had, after all, been insensitive of her feelings for so long. It was hard to expect her now to be solicitous of him.

I held out a hand. 'Good luck.'

'Thanks. Goodbye, Doctor.' She went out the screen door, closing it quietly behind her.

I held the clinic in the store. Afterwards, Gerry led me

proudly towards the homestead. He was rebuilding Invercargill.

'Been working on it round the clock,' he told me. 'The structure's still pretty sound so there's no worries there. Cut the timber for the verandah posts and the roof supports meself. They're bringing the tin in next week.' He led me up the stone steps and into the front door. The outside walls were still blackened with smoke, but on the inside they had been scrubbed clean. 'Have the place finished by the Wet. I reckon Molly won't believe her eyes when she gets back. It'll be like nothing ever happened.'

'Gerry, there's something you ought to know—'

'I've ordered a complete new stock of furniture and of course we'll have to replace all the windows, I'll do the frames meself.'

'Gerry, she's not coming back.'

He stared at me a moment in surprise then pointed to the half-finished lintels. 'Been working nights too with an arc lamp set up over there. She should be out of hospital soon.'

'Gerry, they discharged her last Friday. She came to see me. She said she's not coming back.'

'What are you talking about? 'Course she's comin' back. Where else would she go?'

'She caught the bus to Perth.' For a moment his face crumpled, and I realized with shock that he was on the verge of tears. He turned away from me. 'Gerry . . . ?' I suddenly wanted desperately to be away from there, from Gerry, from the half-finished homestead.

'I'm all right.'

'I'm sorry, Gerry. I really am. I tried to persuade her to come and talk it over with you first. I – I'm sorry.'

Gerry turned back to me and grinned. 'Silly bag. She'll be back.'

'I hope so,' I lied. It wasn't what I hoped for her at

all. Gerry wasn't a bad man, but there wasn't a woman alive who deserved to live with him.

'Eugene will give you and Sam a lift out to the strip,' Gerry said.

I had feared as much, but I said nothing. 'I'll see you next month, Gerry.'

'She'll be back by then,' Gerry said. 'You'll see.'

But Molly didn't come back. Ever. Three months later Gerry Foulkes packed Eugene off to his brother in Mount Isa and started drinking. The tin still hadn't arrived.

One day, Gerry sat himself down in the middle of the half-finished homestead, drained a bottle of Johnnie Walker, and sent all his men into town for the weekend. Then he had a last cigarette, put a stick of dynamite in his mouth, and lit the fuse.

31

The Wet Season. From around the middle of October the days begin to grow hotter. Black storms build during the afternoon, only to fade again at night. The heat and the tension becomes almost unbearable, and sometimes the air is so still a candle will burn outside without flickering. Then, as lightning dances and crackles up the sky, a whistling, moaning thunder breaks across the land from the north-east and the first rains begin to fall, not gently, but in a sudden, crashing deluge.

The Wet has begun. Four months of humid, overcast days and torrential monsoon, of rainstorms hammering like nails on tin roofs, and everywhere the familiar drip, drip, drip of rain falling from the eaves. The black sky flickers with awesome electrical storms as the thunderheads break.

Everything is plastered in orange, sticky mud. Red lakes form in the roads. George's emu, Ethel, adored the first storms. She tiptoed to the puddles like a fussy maiden aunt at the beach. She would test the mud with her beak, then spread her wings, bend the long stalks of her legs and lower herself gently into the water to cool off.

For everyone else, the Wet was something simply to be endured. There is a plague of every kind of flying pest. During daylight the flies harry you and at night mosquitoes hum and dance and seek out warm flesh. Frogs infest the toilets.

The cattle stations are isolated for weeks at a time as rivers flood their banks, and dry watercourses are transformed almost overnight into raging torrents of brown, swirling water. Airstrips become unserviceable and emergency medical evacuations often require the greatest ingenuity.

I was in the middle of the afternoon clinics when the call came in.

'This is Six Victor Sarah, Brookton. We have an emergency. Over.' I recognized Art Johnson's voice.

'Yairs, everyone off the air, please.' Clyde drawled. 'We have an emergency. Go ahead, please, Art.' Clyde turned the transceiver to 'receive' and pushed the mike towards me.

'It's Miss Hoagan,' Art said. 'We were out mustering and her horse fell on her.'

I felt my heart leap into my mouth, but I tried to sound as calm as possible. 'What's her condition, Art? Over.'

'She's in a lot of pain. Her right leg's bust, for sure, and maybe her back too. We don't want to move her.'

'How far is she from the homestead, Art?'

'Couple of hours on a good horse. The creeks are rising and we can't get any of the trucks through.'

'All right, Art, we're on our way. We'll call again when we're in the air.'

A white fog of cloud swallowed the tiny Cessna. Occasionally we glimpsed the ground below us, the rich, red earth shimmering with pools of water. Joe banked to avoid the jagged black edges of another storm front, and the aircraft bucketed and rolled on the turbulence.

As usual, Joe was an inspiration. 'Say your prayers,' he said gloomily. 'We probably won't ever get seen again. We'll vanish like Glenn Miller and Amelia Erhardt.'

'We've been out in worse than this.'

'That's what I mean. Our luck's sure to run out soon.'

I raised Brookton again on the radio. 'Flying Doctor to Six Victor Sarah Brookton. Can you read me? Over.'

'Six Victor Sarah Brookton. Standing by.' The storm whined and hissed over the carrier wave.

'Joe wants to talk to you, Art. Just a moment.'

'G'day,' Joe said. 'What condition's your strip in?'

'She'll do,' Art said. 'Had one of the boys check her out.' Brookton had a good all-weather strip, one of the best in the Kimberley. It could dry out in four hours after even the heaviest downpour. 'What's your ETA?'

'ETA eighteen hundred.' He flicked off the transmit button and turned to me. 'If we get there, that is.'

'I'll have Mitch and Tommy waiting for you in the 'Rover,' Art said.'I'll meet you at the homestead with the horses.'

The flight seemed to take for ever. I thought of Megan and what a mess we'd made of things. I suddenly realized I didn't want to be apart from her again. It was the only thing that mattered. Neither of us had been honest with each other, or with ourselves. Her station and my career, had been convenient excuses for both of us. It prevented us from making a commitment. It was a strange kind of freedom that kept me anchored to a past I had tried to leave behind, and enslaved Megan to her father's dream.

Joe must have read my thoughts. 'Don't worry. She'll be all right.'

'I hope so.'

'It's us I'm worried about. Me, in particular.'

'Just fly the damned plane.'

The light was fading as we came out of the clouds. A network of tracks across the ground converged on the huddle of buildings surrounding the homestead. As we roared over, I glimpsed the familiar white-painted 'BROOKTON' sign on one of the sheds. A few minutes later we landed at the airstrip. The rain was still falling in a steady drizzle and the tyres threw up a curtain of spray.

Sean was waiting for us in the Land-rover. He drove

towards us, braking hard a few feet away from Joe, the tyres throwing up a shower of rainwater and mud. Joe groaned and looked down at his uniform. It was splattered with red goo.

I tried to look sympathetic. 'Just your luck,' I murmured.

'Luck had nothing to do with it,' he said, glaring at Sean. 'The bastard did it deliberately.'

I stood in the shelter of the verandah with Art Johnson, Joe Kennedy and Sean.

'How did it happen?' I asked.

Art took off his hat and beat it against his thigh to shake off the rain. 'We were trying to get the cattle to the higher ground. Her horse shied at a snake, stumbled, and rolled on top of her. Broke its leg. We had to shoot it. Made Miss Hoagan as comfortable as we could then I rode back here on my own. Left the other men with her.'

'How long will it take to get out there?'

'Three hours on a horse. There's three creeks between the homestead and the bore. The water's rising fast. There's no way we can take the vehicles.'

I turned to Sean. 'What about the helicopter?'

'Grounded. I'm still waiting for spares.'

I swore under my breath. 'Just when we needed it.'

'Sod's law,' Joe said. 'If anything can foul up, it will always happen when you need it most.'

'Horses it is then,' I said. I struggled into the poncho Art had brought for me, and slipped the broad-rimmed hat on my head. 'How do I look?'

'Like a city boy trying to be John Wayne,' Joe said. His spirits had lifted since it had become clear he would be staying behind for this one.

'Me and Sean'll go with you,' Art said. 'Mitch'll lead the way.' He nodded towards one of the native stockmen. 'He hasn't got eyes, he's got radar.'

It was almost dark when we climbed on the horses. Art strapped a lightweight stretcher and a wooden board to the side of his mount. I was led to a large bay roan called Butcher. The rain was still falling, dripping from the brims of our stetsons, and I could feel a cold trickle of water leaking down the back of my neck.

Sean leaned across to me. 'Take it easy with that horse. If he doesn't like you, he'll throw you off. They don't call him Butcher for nothing.'

'Thanks.'

We set off across the muddy paddock, through the eucalypts, ghost-green in the pale half-light. The horses' hooves made sucking noises as they trotted through the mud, the ground covered ankle deep in water. It was going to be a long night.

During the winter months, Corrigan's Creek was dry. Now, with the first sudden downpour of the Wet season, it had been transformed into a dark rushing torrent of water, more than twenty feet wide. The night was black, the moon hidden behind the thunderclouds. I could barely make out the silhouettes of the ghost gums along the banks, but I could hear the roar of the water.

Art turned to me. 'Give Butcher plenty of rein. Don't worry, he'll find his own way across.'

'Just don't fall off,' Sean whispered. 'If you do, you're a goner. But try not to think about that.'

The banks of the creek were slick-smooth, and Butcher scrambled side-on down the bank. I clung desperately to the beast's neck, knowing that if he fell we would both slide into the river. Finally, we were in the water and wading across. I could just make out Mitch ahead of me, the water rising quickly to his horse's flanks. I closed my eyes and hung on.

'How much further, Mitch?'

I was soaked, wet with sweat and miserable. We had

forded three creeks, and twice Butcher had stumbled in the water and I had thought we were gone. Each time he somehow managed to steady himself and wade to the other side.

It was still raining.

I leaned forward in the saddle. 'How much further, Mitch?' I repeated.

'Mebbe little bit long way mebbe little bit more bimeby,' Mitch answered.

Armed with this information I plodded on behind him. We were riding Indian file, Sean behind me, Art taking up the rear.

'Mitch, are we lost?'

'No, can't be lost,' Mitch told me. Then he added, with indisputable logic. 'Must be somewhere.'

For a moment the moon appeared from behind the black anvil of a stormcloud. The dark and flat plain spread around us, an endless panorama of silent gums and malee, and the gruesome writhing branches of the boabs. I couldn't believe that anyone, not even Mitch, could find their way in this wilderness on such a night.

I thought of Megan and felt the rising tide of panic.

'Nearly there, Mitch?'

The lights of the camp were dead ahead of us, two bright white specks that seemed to dance on the darkness like fireflies. Mitch turned in his saddle and grinned. 'Number three bore,' he said simply.

'You're a bloody gun, Mitch,' Art murmured.

The four men with Megan had made a camp. Somehow they had managed to get a fire going. The other light came from a hurricane lamp hanging from a branch under one of the gums.

Megan was lying where she had fallen. Her horse lay a few feet away, a still and black silhouette. The men had slid a groundsheet under Megan's body and slipped two sleeping bags under her to support her. She was conscious, but in the light of the lamp she looked deathly pale.

I bent on one knee to examine her. Her eyes flickered open. I smiled. 'It's okay. The doc's here.'

I had been expecting a murmured sigh of relief, but those illusions were soon shattered. 'About time,' Megan hissed. 'Where the hell have you been? I've been lying here for hours.'

'Got here as fast as I could.'

She closed her eyes. 'Christ, it hurts Mike.'

'We'll soon have you fixed up.'

'Don't lie. Just give me a shot of something.'

Her pulse was weak and rapid. I gave her a hundred milligrams of pethidine for the pain and examined her. I was relieved to find no open wound. I felt along her thigh, and the pelvis and the vertebra. There was a break in the femur near the knee. She would have been in excruciating pain for hours.

Art bent over my shoulder. 'Bad?'

'Bad enough.'

'My back's broken, isn't it?' Megan whispered.

'Not as far as I can tell. Your leg is though.'

Art held out a cup of hot, sweet tea. 'See if she can get this down her, eh?'

I held Megan's head and put the cup to her lips. She sipped some down, gratefully. 'No brandy?'

'You have to be really sick before you get brandy,' I told her.

Beyond the shadows of the fire the cattle lowed and fidgeted in the scrub. 'They'll have to take their chances now,' Art said.

I turned my attention to Megan. All I could do was prevent movement of the broken bones, and keep her as free of pain as possible. Sean and Art helped me lift Megan gently onto the stretcher. I slipped the wooden board underneath her, splinted her legs with Kramer wire, and padded her body with cotton wool and bandages.

'We'll take it in turns with the stretcher.'

'Eight fit blokes here, Doc,' Art said. 'No worries there. But we'd better get going as soon as we can. We still have to get back across those creeks.'

'How will we get her across?'

'We've got some canvas in the packs. We can float her across.'

The image of trying to swim the swollen creeks with a stretcher horrified me. But there seemed to be no other choice. 'Okay,' I said. 'Let's go.'

It was an hour after dawn when we reached Corrigan's Creek. A dirty light had crept grudgingly up the eastern sky, smudged with rain. The men slumped to the ground, exhausted.

We had travelled through the night, taking thirty-minute shifts at the stretcher, sloshing through ankle-deep mud. Progress had been painfully slow. We had floated the stretcher across the creeks on the canvas, three men at each side, wading, half-swimming the stretcher to the other side. I had insisted on going across each time. After all, she was my girl. It had forced Sean to make each crossing, too. His pride couldn't allow it to happen any other way.

I bent down beside Megan. 'How are you feeling?'

'My God, Mike, you ask some dumb questions sometimes.'

'Is the pain bad?'

She nodded. Her face was drawn and white from pain and exhaustion. I prepared another shot of pethidene.

'We'll never get her across that, you know.'

Corrigan's Creek, swollen with floodwater, rolled and pitched through the gully in a brown, swirling cascade. It seemed inconceivable that we had crossed it just a few hours before. Art walked over, his brown face creased into a frown. 'The creek's risen during the night. I'm sending Mitch across to check it out. But I think the current's too strong to wade over.'

We watched Mitch's horse, Charlie, scrambling and slipping down the bank. He splashed sideways into the water and for a moment Mitch lost his grip on the reins.

'Shit, he's gone,' Art breathed.

But somehow he regained his balance and as Charlie waded gallantly in, Mitch was still astride him, clinging to his flank, half out of the saddle. Soon the water had reached Charlie's head and he began to swim, Mitch hanging grimly to the rein and bridle. The current carried them fifty yards downstream. Finally the plucky horse scrambled up the far bank, his flanks heaving with exertion.

'Shit,' Art said, shaking his head. 'We're buggered.'

'Looks like it.'

'Head back to the homestead,' Art shouted across the river to Mitch. 'Tell them we're stuck here!'

Mitch waved and trotted off through the paddock towards Brookton.

'Now what?' I asked.

'I dunno. The impossible can be arranged immediately. Miracles take a bit longer.'

He had barely finished speaking when I heard the familiar chop-chop of an engine in the distance. Sean was the first to get to his feet. 'Dust-off,' he shouted.

'What?'

'It's what they called the first-aid choppers in Vietnam. You can't mistake the sound of a helicopter anywhere.'

We scanned the sky eagerly. The ceiling of grey, suffocating cloud seemed to hang just a few feet above us. The sound of the helicopter was coming from the north, and the homestead was to the east. Who was it? We waited.

Suddenly it appeared, about a quarter of a mile away,

flying low over the trees. We immediately took off our hats and waved, yelling frantically to attract the pilot's attention. At once the chopper veered towards us and made a low sweeping pass. It circled once and made its landing in the soft mud about fifty yards away.

The pilot leaned out and waved to Sean.

'It's Neil Brooke,' Sean shouted. 'Works for Banjo.'

Neil turned off the motor, climbed out of the bubble-shaped cockpit and set off in a crouching run under the rotors towards us. 'G'day, Sean, how ya doin', Art?' He was a young man, with an easy-going grin and short bristled hair.

'Well, you're a welcome sight round here,' Art grunted.

'Yeah, that's what all the girls say,' Neil said. He looked at Megan and the grin fell away. 'How is she?'

'Not great.' I told him.

'Boss heard you were having some trouble over the radio. He sent me off this morning to look for you.'

'How did you find us?'

'Wasn't hard. Just followed the creek. I figured if you weren't stuck by any of the gullies, you probably didn't need me anyway.'

'That was smart.'

'Yeah, it was, wasn't it?' Neil said. It seemed humility wasn't the strong suit of helicopter pilots. 'How are we going to shift her?'

'I've seen pictures of how they moved the wounded in Korea,' Sean said. 'They had a stretcher mounted on the helicopter landing struts. We should be able to fix up the same sort of job with some rope.'

'That doesn't sound very safe.'

'I could always leave her here and go home.' Neil said.

He'd made his point. 'All right,' I said. 'Let's get the rope.'

*

Megan lay on the oak kitchen table at Brookton, her leg splinted, a plasma drip feeding into her arm. The rain had stopped. It was just ten o'clock but already the morning was suffocatingly hot. I took a syringe from the medical kit. 'I'll give you a sixth of morphia. It will help you sleep.'

Megan nodded, too weak to speak. The door opened. It was Sean. 'How is she?'

'She'll be better when we get her to the hospital.'

'The rain's holding off. Another couple of hours and the strip should be okay.'

'Good.'

Sean took off his hat and shook off the rain onto the kitchen floor. He went to the table and stood at Megan's side. 'Megan?'

She opened one eye and groaned. 'Oh, it's you,' she whispered.

'I got you back okay,' Sean told her, neatly dismissing the assistance of the rest of us.

'Thank you, Sean,' Megan murmured.

'Something I want to clear up before you go.'

'What is it?'

'It's just that . . . well, while you're away . . . Well, you want to make sure the place is run right . . . Do I take it you're leaving me in charge?'

Megan's body stiffened. She made a futile effort to sit up, then sank back on to the table. 'Get out of here, you cretin,' she hissed.

Sean looked up at me, puzzled. 'Must be all the drugs you're giving her.' He put the hat back on his head and went outside.

I put the needle into her arm. 'It's okay. This will help ease the pain until you're strong enough to fire him,' I said.

'Thanks, Mike,' she murmured, and sank into a deep sleep.

32

A few weeks after Megan's accident, the Fitzroy burst
its banks near Brookton flooding an area of hundreds
of square miles. One night the homestead disappeared
under six feet of water and the men had to retreat to
makeshift camps on higher ground. Thousands of cattle
drowned. I remember flying over the station a few days
later and seeing the obscenely bloated bodies of the
steers floating on the floodwaters or stranded, stiffly
grotesque, in the high branches of the eucalypts.

Then one night a cyclone swept down the north-west
coast, and swept inland along the Dampier peninsula.
We lost contact with Parrot Island.

As soon as the storm had passed Joe and I set off in
the Cessna. When we flew over the island we found
that the tiny settlement had been destroyed, and the
rain tanks swept away by the onslaught of the hurricane. The next day we dropped emergency supplies
onto the island but a week later the first of the Parrot
Island community began to straggle into Preston.

A few weeks later the island was once more deserted.

I drove through the mango and poinciana trees to the
entrance of the hospital. I saw Tom and waved. He
was sitting on the verandah in a wicker chair, watching
the rain. It was moist, sticky hot and the skies were
heavy and molten grey. I leaped out of the Holden and
dashed for the shelter of the verandah.

'How are you, young fella?'

'Not bad, Tom. How are you feeling?'

'All right.' He nodded to the wicker chair beside
him. 'Sit down and tell me your troubles.'

Tom's right hand was still swathed in bandages, and he looked strangely old and frail in the hospital pyjamas. He removed his thick spectacles clumsily with his left hand, and wiped them on the shirt of the pyjamas.

'You've heard about the island?'

'One of the old men came to see me yesterday.'

'I'm sorry.'

'It's not done yet. He said they might go back in a couple of months.'

'Do you think they will?'

He shrugged. 'Who knows? The launch sunk too, you know.'

'Yes.'

'Don't look so bloody miserable. You'll have me crying in a minute.'

'How's the hand?'

'I'll get by. Have to pray one-handed in future.' He forced a smile.

'You'll be out of here soon.'

'Yes. They reckon they might fit me with a hook. Be handy for fishing.' We were silent for a while, staring at the rain. 'I don't know what's going to become of those people, Mike,' he said after a while. 'Blokes like me are partly to blame. Stuffing our religion down their throats. The older I get, the more I come to realize that there wasn't much wrong with the religion they already had.'

'I thought you were trying to convert them.'

'I gave that up years ago. In the last ten years I've only baptized two, and one of them reverted.' He scratched irritably at a nest of mosquito bites on his neck. 'As soon as the Wet's over I'm going back, Mike. The old men will come back too. I know it.'

'Anything I can do to help?'

'I'll let you know.'

245

I instinctively held out my hand. He grinned and shook hands left-handed. 'Take care,' I told him.

'I'll see you around, young fella,' he said. 'That reminds me, I must get a new pair of glasses.' He took off his spectacles and impulsively threw them in the bushes. 'Can't see a bloody thing through them.'

Of all the Kimberley towns, Broome is the one that most stirs the spirit. It is haunted by the ghosts of a rich and romantic past. The town had been born just eighty-five years before as a huddle of mosquito-infested tents on the red sandhills overlooking Roebuck Bay. Within a few years it became the pearling centre of the world, producing gems that were sought after by the high society of London, Paris and Berlin.

The port was lawless and untamed, and the pearlers – adventurers who came to the north-west seeking their fortunes – lived by their own rules. In its short history Broome witnessed cyclones, racial riots and war-time bombing raids by the Japanese. The brief glorious years came to an end during the nineteen fifties after a crash in the market for mother-of-pearl.

During its heyday there was no other town like it in Australia. The majority of its population came from south-east Asia. Hundreds of Japanese and Koepangers were indentured to the industry to work on the pearling boats, the Japanese being regarded as best suited for the brutal demands of the work. The diver would be in the water at dawn, and the day's work would not end until sunset. Dressed in heavy lead boots, diving suit and sea-greened copper helmet, each driver would grope through the murky world of the seabed, the bag of shell slung round his neck, the pressure creasing and pinching his heavy canvas suit.

No one understood then about decompression sickness – commonly known as the 'bends'. At depth nitrogen is absorbed into the bloodstream; if the pressure is released suddenly, the nitrogen fizzes in the blood like soda water, causing paralysis or an agonizing death.

Most of the divers suffered from 'rheumatics' in the joints, associated with decompression sickness. Many, after spending all day in the water, were kept awake all night by the pain. A major attack could leave them writhing on the deck, helpless and in excrutiating agony. Sometimes the only relief for the diver was to climb again into the still-wet canvas suit, and be lowered once again into the pitch-black sea.

Between 1910 and 1917, 145 divers died from 'diver's paralysis'. Many more were sent back to their homelands to live out the rest of their days as beggars, crippled for life. An advertisement preserved in Broome Museum, printed on the back of a 1913 programme for a travelling vaudeville show, illustrates just what a risky business it was:

PUBLIC NOTICE TO DIVERS
Why live when you can die and be buried for £7 10s?
No waiting, no delay. First come, first served.
10% reduction for a quantity.

THE HURRY MOTOR UNDERTAKING COMPANY

It wasn't until 1913, and the introduction of the first steel decompression chamber – together with the introduction of navy decompression tables – that the scourge was finally brought under control.

The Japanese cemetery in Broome still bears silent testimony to how many of the divers lost their lives in the search for the precious shells. There are row upon row of graves, the headstones fashioned from coloured beach rock, mute witness to the deadly effects of the bends. There is also a memorial to the men who drowned at sea, and whose bodies were never found. Since the luggers relied on sail, they were often caught in the 'calm of the storm' that precedes a tropical cyclone. In the 'blows' of 1887 and 1935 140 men were drowned.

Broome was a town where fortunes were won and lost overnight. There is a story of a pearler who once found the biggest pearl ever seen in Broome; it weighed 264 grains. It had one small blemish, however, and this was enough to make it worthless. The man brought the pearl to Tom Ellies, a Sinhalese pearl cleaner, reputed to be the best in Broome. Tom's profession was to 'peel' the pearls, as if peeling an onion. Sometimes a blemish might clean away with first skin. That afternoon Tom peeled away layer after layer but the blemish remained. Finally the pearl lay in shavings on his desk. The pearler had walked in the door with a possible fortune in his hands. When he walked out again, he had nothing.

When war broke out in 1941 the Japanese population of Broome exceeded the European. The day after Pearl Harbour, one European, Sam Male, walked down to the crowds of Japanese on the beach and told them they were to be interned. They could have easily massacred the whites in the town, but there was only docile compliance. After all, they had all been friends for years. They were led off to the jail by one young soldier with a rifle.

Three months later the situation was much different. A squadron of Zeros made a surprise raid on Broome and found sixteen flying boats below them in Roebuck Bay, their crews enjoying a final drink in the Continental Hotel. Many of the flying boats were crammed with women and children, refugees from the Japanese advance in Java. The Zeros swooped down, their cannons blazing.

There has never been an official casualties list but

the number of dead is reckoned to have been at least a hundred. In the smoke-blackened chaos of Roebuck Bay the women and children who had survived the machine-guns of the Zeros tried to swim for the beach and were taken by sharks.

Even today, when there is a low tide the rusting hulks of three of the Dorniers can still be seen, remarkably well preserved among the sandbanks. They rest silently in the mud, home now for a colony of rustling crabs, the drama and tragedy that made Broome their final graves now almost forgotten.

But that day brought one other incident that has not been forgotten on the Dampier Peninsula. As the Zeros flew back to their base on Koepang, they crossed the path of an unarmed DC–3 flying towards Broome. It was a Dutch civilian plane, carrying refugees from Bandoeng in Java.

The plane was shot down, crash-landing in Carnot Bay to the north of Broome. The survivors waded ashore to the beach. After their rescue, the pilot, an expatriate Russian called Ivan Smirnoff, was questioned about a parcel that had been thrown on the plane as he was taxi-ing away from the airstrip at Bandoeng. Unknown to him or the crew, the parcel had contained a quarter of a million pounds in diamonds. Naturally, the pilot shrugged away the questions; struggling to beach his crippled plane and with five bullet wounds in his arms, the unmarked brown paper parcel in the plane's safe had been the last thing on his mind.

But now, some twenty-five years later, there were some people who could think of nothing else.

It was near the end of the Wet. I went to see Clyde, to tell him I was planning to take a weekend off, and drive down to Broome.

'Yairs, going to take a few days off meself,' Clyde

said, 'Me and Gordon are going camping up the Dampier peninsula. Take the old Land-rover.'

'Looking for anything in particular?'

Clyde lowered his voice – an unnecessary precaution in the steamy solitude of the radio hut – and leaned forward. 'Darn well forgot.'

'What?'

'It's the key. Me and Gordon have figured it out.'

'Figured what out?'

'He didn't say "darn well forgot" at all.'

'Yes he did. I was there.'

'Yairs, well, that wasn't what he meant.' The fat and hairy caterpillars of Clyde's eyebrows wriggled once in some arcane code unknown to me.

'Clyde, I've no idea what you're talking about.'

'Cape Fourget. It's twenty miles north of Carnot. There must be a well up there. That's where the diamonds are hidden. "Down – well – Fourget." That's what Jim was trying to tell you.'

'You have a vivid imagination.'

Clyde sniffed, and turned back to the radio, preparing for the morning skeds. I had offended him. 'We'll see.'

The road down to Broome is arrow straight and deadly monotonous stretching for mile after mile across the pindan scrub and flatlands. It's known as Tombstone Flats, because of the profusion of tomb-like termite mounds that dot the scrub, and had just re-opened after the Wet. Everywhere there were road gangs busily repairing those sections that had been destroyed by the Fitzroy floodwaters.

I arrived in Broome early in the afternoon and drove along Dampier Terrace, to the Continental Hotel. The old hotel was a relic from Broome's heyday, with its wide, shaded verandahs overhung with purple bougainvillaea, creaking cedar floors and gently whirring over-

250

head fans. I found Megan sitting on the verandah outside her room, reading a magazine. Her leg, still encased in plaster, was stretched in front of her, and a pair of crutches were resting against the wall. She was wearing white shorts and a pink cotton blouse, and her left leg and her arms were tanned a honey brown. On the station she always wore her hair braided behind her head but now it fell heavily around her shoulders. She looked wonderful.

'Long John Silver, I presume?'

She looked up in surprise, and then her face split into a huge grin. 'Mike!' She tried to get to her feet.

I leaned across and put my hand on her shoulders. 'You're supposed to rest, Doctor's orders.'

She grabbed the hair at the back of my neck and pulled me towards her. She kissed me long and hard on the mouth. 'What are you doing here?'

'I came to see you. I've got the weekend off.'

'You've never taken a weekend off before.'

'You've never broken your leg before.'

'Is that all I have to do to get your attention? You should have told me before.'

I sat down on the verandah rail. 'We have to talk. This time I have something to say.'

The old lugger, *Sam Male*, lay on its side in the mud at the end of the jetty. We stood on the creaking timber boards, looking out across the creek towards the sea. Below us the little orange mud crabs kept up their incessant clicking and rustling around the roots of the mangroves.

'They pulled down the long jetty last year,' Megan said. 'The town isn't what it used to be.'

'Everything changes.'

'Yes, it does. What about us. Are we going to change?'

I took a deep breath. 'I've been thinking about that

offer I had. To go back to Sydney, into private practice.'

She forced a smile. 'Are you going to take it?'

'I can't do this job for ever. I don't want to be still wading through creeks when I'm sixty-five.'

She was silent for a while. 'I'm going to sell Brookton.'

'Are you serious?'

'We lost three-quarters of the stock this Wet and the homestead's still under water. I don't think I can go back and start all over again.'

It was what I had wanted to hear her say all along. To my surprise I heard myself saying: 'Of course you can go back. You must.'

She shook her head. 'I want to come with you.'

'You'd hate it. You'd shrivel up and die in the city.'

'I want to be with you.'

I put my hands on her shoulders. I tried to imagine us back in the city, with a brick house and a pool. I tried to imagine myself wearing a suit again and keeping regular hours. I tried to imagine Megan in a supermarket, or in a leather-upholstered sedan instead of a leather-saddled horse. Maybe she could survive there.

But suddenly I realised I couldn't. 'It won't work,' I whispered.

'It has to.'

'No, I'm not going back. I want to wear a hat and ride a horse.'

Megan stared at me, her eyes wide. Then she threw back her head and laughed.

'What's so funny?'

'You want to come and work on Brookton?'

'It seems to be the only solution. I can't leave this place now. I love it too much. The heat, the floods, the mosquitoes, the dust, the hardship. I'm as crazy as the rest of you now.'

'I don't believe it.'

'I'm serious. There's just one condition.'

'What's that?'

'Sean has to go.'

She cocked her head to one side. 'The Gunner too?'

I looked at her in amazement. 'You told me you fired him.'

'I re-hired him. He really does make the best damper I've ever tasted.'

I shook my head. 'I hope this is going to work out.'

The morning sun glinted on the rich and glinting blue of Roebuck Bay. I stood on the verandah in my shorts and took deep lungfuls of the warm-scented air. I was once again a married man.

It had not been easy to arrange, but we had not trusted ourselves to delay the moment any longer. We had found a Justice of the Peace, and the local postmaster, a one-time friend and associate of Megan's father, Jesse, had agreed to be our witness. The ceremony took less than five minutes, I finally committed myself to the Kimberley and to Brookton. It felt good.

A grey-painted Land-rover, its coachwork inch thick with mud, pulled into the car park. I recognized the driver immediately. It was Clyde.

I strolled across and opened the door. 'What are you doing here?'

Clyde jumped out of the cab and gave me a sour look. 'I might ask you the same thing.'

'I'm staying here.'

He grunted. 'With Miss Hoagan, I suppose.'

'That's right.'

He scowled, and slammed shut the driver's door.

'What's wrong with you?' I asked.

'It's immoral, that's what it is.'

'What's immoral?'

'What you're doing is immoral.'

I felt myself getting angry. 'That's good coming from you.'

He straightened, and thrust out his jaw. 'What's that supposed to mean?'

'*I've* not been running all around the Dampier peninsula trying to dig up other people's diamonds!'

'That's not as immoral as what you're doin'!'

'What am I doing?'

'Using up that young girl just whenever you feel like it! I mean . . . I know what it's like when you're . . . well, when you're your age . . . I mean, me and Mary . . . Well, never mind about me and Mary, but I never trifled with her affections like–'

'I didn't trifle with anything! She's got a broken thigh bone, for God's sake!'

'That's worse.'

'Anyway, we got married yesterday.'

Clyde stared at me for a while, sucking noisily at his teeth with his tongue. He scratched at his armpit. 'Yairs, well, that's different.'

'No it isn't. Her leg's still broken.'

'I don't mean that.' He shuffled his feet, embarrassed. 'Jeez, you might have told someone.'

'We were going to.'

'Good job old Jesse's passed on,' he said. 'If he were alive today, he'd be turning in his grave.'

There was a muffled thud from the rear of the Landrover. I peered in through the mud-grimed window. It was Gordon. He was curled up on the bare metal floor, one arm draped around a shovel and his head resting on a jerrican. He was fast asleep. 'Had a few too many at the Roebuck last night,' Clyde explained. 'We was celebratin'.'

'You found some diamonds?'

'Nar, didn't find a cracker. We was celebratin' the

fact that we've given up lookin'. Bloody hard work, it was.'

'You haven't told me what you're doing here.'

'Just on our way back to Preston. Came to say hello to Meg. Didn't expect to see you here as well.'

'Ah well, it's a small world.'

'Oh well, I might as well give you this now then.' He reached into the cab and opened the dashboard locker. He took out a small brown paper envelope.

'This is for you.'

'What is it?'

'Open it and you'll find out.'

I tore open the seal. A gold ring dropped into my palm. The ring had a small white diamond set into it.

'What's this?'

'Picked it up yesterday. There's a bloke I know here used to work for a big jewellers in London. Did a good job, di'n't he?'

'I don't understand.'

'Trouble with you, you're too bloody honest. I knew you'd give the rotten thing back. So I swapped it for the phoney one–'

'You?'

'–so I could do something useful with it. Don't let Mary know where it came from, will ya? I'll never hear the last of it.'

'You broke into my house?'

'No, or course not. What do you think I am, a thief? I got George to get it for me.'

'And I thought it was Dawson.'

'He's not smart enough to think of something like this.'

'Clyde I – I don't know what to say.'

'Just keep quiet about it, that's all. Or we'll all be in the 'nure.' He gave me a long, slow smile. 'Yairs, well, she deserves a decent ring. She's too good for you, but I s'pose you already know that.'

'Thanks.'

'Yairs, well, I guess you'll be leaving us then.'

I nodded. 'Yes.'

'You going to Brookton?'

'Looks like it.'

'Well, don't smile too soon. I reckon your troubles are only just beginning.'